THE SEPTEMBER ISSUE

Anna Wintour
（アナ・ウィンター）

アメリカ版『VOGUE』編集長。3,000億ドルのファッション産業界の最重要人物と言われる。映画『プラダを着た悪魔』でメリル・ストリープが演じた編集長のモデルとしても有名。

Grace Coddington
（グレイス・コディントン）

アメリカ版『VOGUE』のクリエイティブ・ディレクターで、アナ・ウィンターの右腕。ウェールズのアングルシー島出身。元モデル。

Sienna Miller
（シエナ・ミラー）

アメリカ・ニューヨーク生まれ、イギリス・ロンドン育ちのモデル、女優、ファッションデザイナー。

Thakoon Panichgul
（タクーン・パニクガル）

タイ生まれ、ネブラスカ州オマハ育ちの新進デザイナー。ファッションブランドTHAKOONを設立。ニューヨークを拠点に活動する。

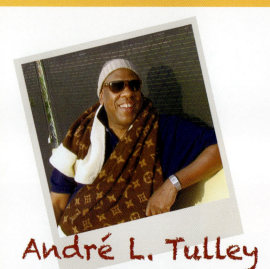

André L. Tulley

（アンドレ・レオン・タリー）
アメリカ版『VOGUE』の総合監修者（editor-at-large）。彼の豪快なテニスプレーも見どころ。

Tonne Goodman

（トニ・グッドマン）
アメリカ版『VOGUE』編集部でファッション・ディレクターを務める。

Charles (Charlie) Churchward

（チャールズ［チャーリー］・チャーチウォード）
アメリカ・ニュージャージー州で育つ。ニューヨークでマガジン・アート・ディレクターとして活躍。アメリカ版『VOGUE』、『VANITY FAIR』のデザイン・ディレクターを歴任。

Raquel Zimmermann

（ラケル・ジマーマン）
ブラジルのファッションモデル。日本とパリで活動。スティーヴン・マイゼル撮影のイタリア版『VOGUE』2000年9月号の表紙で注目を集めたことから、本格的な活動が始まった。

THE SEPTEMBER ISSUE

映画総合教材『ファッションが教えてくれること』

SHOHAKUSHA

■
映画スクリプト作成者：永野和幸
■

THE SEPTEMBER ISSUE
based on the film
directed by R. J. Cutler
Copyright © 2009 by A & E Television Networks LLC
and Awe Entertainment, Inc.
All rights reserved.
This edition published under license from
A & E Television Networks LLC.
日本語版版権代理店：㈱イングリッシュ・エージェンシー ジャパン

映画『ファッションが教えてくれること』

原題	The September Issue
上映時間	90分
製作国	アメリカ
公開	2009年
配給	KlockWorx Co.ltd
監督	R. J. Cutler
製作総指揮	Molly Thompson / Robert DeBitetto / Robert Sharenow

　『ファッションが教えてくれること』は、ファッション誌『VOGUE』で最も重要な9月号の制作を記録したドキュメンタリー映画です。アメリカ版『VOGUE』誌の主幹編集長（editor-in-chief）アナ・ウィンターの動きを追ったこのドキュメンタリーでは、映画が進むにつれ9月号に何を掲載するかの決断がなされていきます。

　アナ・ウィンターは、1949年にイギリスのロンドンでアメリカ人の母とイギリス人の父のもとに生まれます。彼女の家はジャーナリストの家系です。父チャールズ・ウィンターは現在ではロンドンで唯一の夕刊紙となった『ロンドン・イヴニング・スタンダード』の編集者です。アナはその象徴とも言えるボブ・スタイルの髪型、極端に大きなサングラス、生真面目で、ときとして冷酷とも言える仕事のやり方で有名です。アナは1988年から『VOGUE』誌の編集長を務めています。

　このドキュメンタリーに登場する他の重要な人物には、クリエイティブ・ディレクターのグレイス・コディントン、総合監修者（editor-at-large）のアンドレ・レオン・タリー、ファッション・ディレクターのチャールズ（チャーリー）・チャーチウォード、ファッション・デザイナーのタクーン・パニクガルらがいます。

　『ファッションが教えてくれること』はR・J・カトラー監督のもとで製作され、2009年に公開されました。5つの映画賞にノミネートされ、うち2009年サンダンス映画祭撮影監督賞と2010年シネマ・アイ・オナーズ観客特別賞の二つを受賞しました。

　2003年にアナの元助手であったローレン・ワイズバーガーによる小説『プラダを着た悪魔』（The Devil Wears Prada）が出版され、次いで2006年に映画化されました。この作品は、アナと『VOGUE』の主幹編集長としての彼女の豪腕ぶりを描いたものとされています。『プラダを着た悪魔』では、アナに当たる人物はミランダ・プリーストリーという名前になっており、映画ではアメリカの実力派女優メリル・ストリープが演じています。

Table of Contents

1	**2007年ニューヨーク** Culture　毛皮と動物の権利	06
2	**ヴォーグ主催年次朝食会** Grammar　使役表現	12
3	**ヴォーグへの道** Communication Tip　自然な会話術――"like"の様々な使い方	20
4	**タクーン** Culture　写真家ブラッサイ	26
5	**締め切りまで6週間** Grammar　等位接続詞 (coordinating conjunctions)	32
6	**パリへ** Communication Tip　自然な会話術――"Hi"と"Hello"だけではない会話中のあいさつ表現	38
7	**パリ　オートクチュール・コレクション** Culture　映画『ローマの休日』のアン王女の言葉遣い	46
8	**テニスコートのアンドレ** Grammar　動名詞と不定詞	52
9	**グレイスの回想** Communication Tip　自然な会話術――疑問文のイントネーション	58
10	**カラー・ブロッキング テイク2〜エンド・クレジット** Culture　ジャズ・エイジ (Jazz Age)	64

Transcript　　　　　　　　　　　　　　　　　　　　　　　　　71

Previewing Activities

この映画教材で学習する前にグループやペアで意見を交換してみましょう。
いずれかのトピックを選んで行なうのでも構いません。

☐ What role does fashion play in your life? Is fashion something important to you? Why or why not?

_____

☐ Name some fashion designers you are familiar with. Who are some of your favourite fashion designers? What do you like about their fashion style?

_____

☐ What do you know about *Vogue* magazine? Have you ever read it?

_____

☐ Have you ever seen the film *The Devil Wears Prada*? If yes, what did you think about the main character, Miranda Priestly?

_____

Unit 1
2007年ニューヨーク

◇ 本章スクリプト→ P. 71 ～ 76　　*DVD*　Ch. 1　00:00:08-00:08:26

ファッション業界のリーダーたる審美眼を持ち、妥協しない姿勢を貫くアメリカ版『VOGUE』編集長アナ・ウィンター。彼女の決定によってすべてがくつがえり、制作スタッフがどよめくこともしばしば。そんな彼らの仕事ぶりと、『VOGUE』制作の裏側を覗いてみましょう。

| Culture | 毛皮と動物の権利 |

Warming Up
映画を視聴する前に確認しておきましょう

• Vocabulary Check　　　　　　　　 Audio Track 2

映画の場面に出てくる語句を使って、空欄を埋めましょう。必要な場合は語形を変えてください。

```
• insecure    • excluded    • mock       • fired
• industry    • famine      • renowned
```

1. Union leaders believe relationships are important in the airline _____.
2. She is _____ from the board meeting because of what she said.
3. He was criticized for _____ the prime minister's economic recovery plan.
4. Children feel less _____ when they are with their parents.
5. She is internationally _____ for her novels.
6. They got _____ because they stole the company's money.
7. The _____ of cotton struck the textile companies in 18th-century Europe.

Viewing
場面を視聴して内容をつかみましょう

• Comprehension

次の問題の答えを選択肢から選びなさい。正解を示す場面を見て確認してみましょう。

1. 📀 00:02:33-00:02:52

What does Candy mean by "I would say 'Pope'"?

(A) Anna is a rebel in the fashion industry.
(B) Anna is an admirer of Alexander Pope, an 18th-century English poet.
(C) Anna is actually a devout Catholic.
(D) Anna is an authority figure in fashion like the Pope in the Roman Catholic Church.

2. 📀 00:02:58-00:03:17

Tom says, "L'Oréal's meeting Anna to talk about having designers design an infallible dress." In this context, the phrase <u>infallible dress</u> is closest in meaning to

(A) a dress a morally perfect person would wear.
(B) a dress even a critic would think is perfect.
(C) a dress with no holes or no dirt on it.
(D) a dress everyone would like to buy.

3. 📀 00:04:01-00:04:18

The journalists make all the following statements about Anna EXCEPT

(A) Anna is famous as the editor-in-chief of the magazine *Vogue*.
(B) It is believed that people watch Anna more closely than film actors.
(C) Anna's magazine is considered to be a bible for the fashion industry.
(D) Anna earns $300 billion a year.

4. 📀 00:05:38-00:05:49

What does André say about his own role at the défilé?

(A) He helps Anna decide what goes in *Vogue*.
(B) He helps the editors of *Vogue* negotiate with Anna.
(C) He tells the editors of *Vogue* about Anna's decisions.
(D) He tells Anna about the decisions of the editors of *Vogue*.

• **Dictation**

音声を聞いて、シナリオの空所に当てはまる英語を書き入れましょう。

① 📀 00:00:08-00:01:10   🔊 Audio Track 3

Start ▶▶▶

▶▶▶ End

Notes

Anna: I . . . I think what . . . I . . . I often see is that people are 1. _____ of fashion and that . . . because it scares them or makes them feel 2. _____, they put it down. On the 3. _____, people that say demeaning things about . . . uh . . . our world, I think that's usually because they feel, in some ways, 4. _____ or, you know, not part of the cool group or . . . So, as a result, they . . . they just 5. _____ it. Just because you like to put on a beautiful Carolina Herrera dress or a — I don't know — pair of J Brand blue jeans, that you know, instead of something basic from K-Mart, it doesn't mean that you're a . . . a dumb person. There is something about fashion that can make people very 6. _____.

demeaning: 恥ずべき

Carolina Herrera: キャロリーナ・ヘレラ（ベネズエラ出身の母娘デザイナーによるブランド）
J. Brand: アメリカ発のデニム・ブランド
K-Mart: アメリカのディスカウントストア・チェーン
dumb: 物言わぬ ※「役に立たない」を含意する

② 📀 00:06:57-00:08:26   🔊 Audio Track 4

Start ▶▶▶

▶▶▶ End

Anna: Stefano, can we start?
Stefano: Yes. OK. [*chuckles*] Anna. Is this? . . . I'll show them three by three. So, this is look number one. OK, you just walk

three by three : 3点ずつ ※one by one: 一つずつ

	around easily. Voilà. So, this season, basically what I decided to work on is to go back to the 7. _____ of the cut. Everything is hand-stitched, all around.
Hamish:	Wow.
Anna:	I don't see any real evening on that 8. _____. Are you not doing it?
Stefano:	No. I am . . .
Anna:	But?
Stefano:	But they're all . . .
Anna:	In pieces? Do we have sketches?
Stefano:	Yes . . . I have one cocktail dress. But this is the workmanship, which is this one. No. Did you see that, no?
Anna:	No, that's pretty. So, you're not really feeling for color, Stefano.
Stefano:	No. No. No. You know, it's . . . it's . . . it's my 9. _____. I mean, in winter, I never feel so much for color. It's more it's more a summer thing for me, frankly speaking, but . . . it's a bit 10. _____. New . . . blacks. I don't know. There's blue navy. There is . . . there is an emerald green. [*chuckles*] You know.
Anna:	Very colorful.
Stefano:	This is colorful.
Virginia:	Okay, I'm gonna need you when I'm convincing Anna that that's not black. We have green, navy . . .

Voilà: [仏]（注意を引いて）見て、ほら

hand-stitched: 手縫いする

evening=evening dress

cocktail dress: パーティ等で着る婦人服。イブニングドレスよりもカジュアルなものを指す。
workmanship:（職人の）技量

Post-Viewing: Review
発展演習で理解を深めましょう

● Discussion

ペアやグループで意見を交換しましょう。

1. What do you think of Anna's view of fashion?
2. When a journalist asks Anna, "Is there a way to wear fur this winter?" she says, "There is always a way to wear fur. Personally, I have it on my back." This is supposed to be a joke. Why is it funny?
3. Anna complains, "You're not really feeling for color, Stefano." Stefano Pilati says, "in winter, I never feel so much for color." What are your thoughts? Who would you agree with? Why?

Culture
毛皮と動物の権利

　アナ・ウィンターが毛皮について訊かれる場面が登場しますが、欧米ではこの数年、毛皮をめぐって様々な議論がなされていることも知っておくとよいでしょう。「毛皮や皮革製品のために動物を犠牲にすることは倫理に反するのではないか」という議論があり、とりわけ若い人たちに支持が広がっています。

　欧米で毛皮や皮革製品のために動物を殺すことに抵抗を覚える人が多くなったのは、動物がかわいそうという感情的な理由からだけではありません。「苦痛を感じることのできる動物であれば、彼らにも不必要な苦痛から逃れる権利があるのではないか」という考え方が普及しているからです。この「苦痛を感じられる能力」のことを、英語では"sentience"（形容詞は"sentient"）と言います。この考えを提唱した有名なアメリカの思想家がピーター・シンガーです。彼は著書『動物の権利』(*Animal Liberation*, 1975) で、こう述べています。

① 日本語に訳してみましょう。
If a being suffers there can be no moral justification for refusing to take that suffering into consideration.

　動物の権利について、もっとラディカルな考え方を持つ人もいます。南アフリカのノーベル賞作家J・M・クッツェーは、『動物のいのち』(*The Lives of Animals*, 1999) という講演の中で、架空の小説家エリザベス・コステロにこのように言わせます。

② 日本語に訳してみましょう。
To me, a philosopher who says that the distinction between human and nonhuman depends on whether you have a white or a black skin, and a philosopher who says that the distinction between human and nonhuman depends on whether or not you know the difference between a subject and a predicate, are more alike than they are unlike.

Notes　subject: 主語　predicate: 述語

イギリスのデザイナー、ステラ・マッカートニーはヴェジタリアンであるのみならず、毛皮やレザーの使用に反対する動物の権利（"animal rights"）を推進する運動家としても有名で、動物の殺戮を伴わない製品を作ることで有名です。1994年にはアメリカのカルヴァン・クライン、2006年にはラルフ・ローレン、2008年にはトミー・ヒルフィガー、2015年にはドイツのヒューゴ・ボスが毛皮の廃止を決定し、2016年3月にはイタリアのジョルジョ・アルマーニも毛皮廃止を発表しました。

　ファッションの中心地フランスでもこうした動物の権利についての議論がなされており、金銭的理由ではなく道徳的理由からフェイク・ファーを選ぶ人が多くいます。2015年12月25日放送のFrance 2のニュースでは、上質のフェイク・ファーのほうが本物の毛皮よりも人気があり、フランスの製品検査機関であるEmitechの調査でも保温効果がほぼ変わらなくなったと報道されています。

● Research Activities

現在のファッションにおける毛皮や皮革製品の状況を調べてみましょう。日本で広く知られているブランドやショップにも、毛皮製品の取り扱いをやめたところがたくさんあります。

Unit 2
ヴォーグ主催年次朝食会

◇ 本章スクリプト→ P. 77 〜 84　　DVD　Ch. 2　00:08:27-00:17:14

アナとスタッフたちは、小売業者との年次朝食会に参加します。今季の服のポイントなどが話題にあがるなか、ニーマンマーカス社 CEO のバートン・タンスキーは、あることでアナに協力を求めます。それはアナには一見関係なさそうな内容ですが……

Grammar　　使役表現

Warming Up
映画を視聴する前に確認しておきましょう

• Vocabulary Check　　 Audio Track 5

映画の場面に出てくる語句を使って、空欄を埋めましょう。必要な場合は語形を変えてください。

> • ignite　• reinterpret　• purview　• outstrip
> • dissect　• clinical　• withstand　• bionic

1. The Cabinet pushed to _____ the war-renouncing Article 9 of the Constitution.

2. All buildings must be able to _____ an earthquake of upper 6 or greater on the Japanese scale.

3. A decisive war against Iraq could _____ terrorist attacks.

4. The mad scientist transformed Logan into a _____ man.

5. My question might fall within the _____ of your expertise.

6. The race car driver managed to drive a superb race to _____ all other drivers.

7. I wouldn't stay there again because the room was very white and _____ which made me so uneasy that I couldn't sleep a wink.

8. If you _____ the movie scene by scene, you will find many flaws.

Notes　Cabinet: 内閣　war-renouncing: 戦争放棄の　decisive war: 決戦　expertise: 専門知識　flaw: 不備

Viewing

場面を視聴して内容をつかみましょう

● Comprehension

次の問題の答えを選択肢から選びなさい。正解を示す場面を見て確認してみましょう。

1. DVD 00:09:08-00:09:18

What does Tom mean by "If we get behind something, it sells"?

(A) The key to selling clothes is to have a large stock of clothes.
(B) *Vogue* sells well when it has a stock of clothes.
(C) What *Vogue* features is what will become popular.
(D) Anna is the force behind *Vogue*.

2. DVD 00:09:51-00:10:51

What does Burton mean by "you'll look like a telephone book this year"?

(A) This year's September issue will be an issue that everyone has at home like a telephone book.
(B) This year's September issue will be very thick like a telephone book.
(C) This year's September issue will likely feature all the brands that people need to know.
(D) This year's September issue will be as simple as a telephone book.

3. DVD 00:13:19-00:13:32

Candy says, "This is when I say, I'm gonna try to get back on those high heels, 'cause, okay, that's the look." In this context, the phrase <u>the look</u> is closest in meaning to

(A) how you look.
(B) the latest trend.
(C) what people normally wear in September.
(D) what makes me look good.

4. DVD 00:13:35-00:13:45

What does Grace mean by "Well, it's a story crying to be done"?

(A) It is a sad story that you cannot help crying.
(B) It is a story that is very hard to edit.
(C) It is a story that was already featured in a previous issue.
(D) It is a story that we should include in the issue.

● Dictation

音声を聞いて、シナリオの空所に当てはまる英語を書き入れましょう。

① 📀 00:12:14-00:12:49　　　　　　　　　　　　　🔊 Audio Track 6

Start ▶▶▶　　　▶▶▶ End

Notes

Tom: When we put out the September issue of *Vogue*, the first thing the reporters usually ask us is how much does it 1. _____ and how many pages?
2. _____ _____ _____ American 3. _____ , almost thirteen million people, will get that issue. A few years ago when we put out a record issue of September, it was the largest monthly magazine ever published. Guys, we're looking to break that record. We have to break 4. _____ _____ . I want you to go into it like it's *Vogue* the brand and market it like it's never been 5. _____ in its entire 114 years.

② 00:15:33-00:15:56 Audio Track 7

Grace: You have to learn the way to 6. _____ your path through to make yourself 7. _____ and make yourself necessary and find a way that works for you, for *Vogue* because a lot of people have come and a lot of people have gone. They just couldn't take the 8. _____ . You know, you have to be 9. _____ tough to 10. _____ that.

Post-Viewing: Review
発展演習で理解を深めましょう

● Discussion

ペアやグループで意見を交換しましょう。

1. Tom says, "Nobody was wearing fur until Anna put it back on the cover of *Vogue* back in the early nineties, and she ignited the entire industry. If we get behind something, it sells." Obviously, Anna is one of the most influential women in fashion. How? Also, try to think of the most influential person in another field and explain why you think this person is so.
2. When Burton raises a problem about deliveries of merchandise, Anna does not take it seriously because she is the Editor-in-Chief of *Vogue* and not a truck driver, so that she thinks there is nothing she can do. However, Burton's cry for help is serious and Anna takes it seriously after she listens. What is the problem?
3. Candy says "September is the January in fashion, you know? This is when I change. This is when I say, I'm gonna try to get back on those high heels, 'cause, okay, that's the look." Think about why September is considered the beginning of a new year for the fashion industry.

Grammar
使役表現

Grace: You have to learn the way to beat your path through to make yourself felt and make yourself necessary and find a way that works for you, for *Vogue* because a lot of people have come and a lot of people have gone.

　使役表現と言えば、≪使役動詞＋目的語＋原形不定詞≫の形をまず思い浮かべると思いますが、時に≪使役動詞＋目的語＋過去分詞≫の形で現れる場合があります。前者は、「～に…させる」、「～に…してもらう」という意味を持ち、後者は「～を…された状態にする」、「～を…された状態にしてもらう［させる］」という意味を持ちます。なぜこのような違いが生じるのか見ていきましょう。

　使役動詞の代表的なものとしてよく挙げられるのは、make, have, let です。これらの動詞は強制の度合いが異なり、強制の度合いは、make ＞ have ＞ let となります。この順番で覚えておくと良いでしょう。

　次に、原形不定詞を取る場合と過去分詞を取る場合の違いについてです。ここでは例として have を用いて説明します。

　　(1) I had a professional <u>paint</u> the walls.
　　(2) I had the walls <u>painted</u> (by a professional).

(1) は原形不定詞 paint を伴った文、(2) は過去分詞 painted を伴った文です。どちらの文も「プロの職人に壁をペンキで塗ってもらった。」という意味の文です。それぞれの文の使役動詞 have 以下の要素だけに注目して見てみましょう。

　　(3) a professional <u>paint</u> the walls
　　(4) the walls <u>painted</u> (by a professional)

これらを比べると、原形不定詞の場合と過去分詞の場合で違いがはっきり見て取れます。(3) は動詞 paint が主語 a professional と目的語 the walls を持つ能動文のようであり、(4) はその受動文のようになっています。(3) と (4) を文にすると、(5) と (6) のようになります。

　　(5) A professional <u>painted</u> the walls.
　　(6) The walls were <u>painted</u> (by a professional).

このように考えると、使役動詞 have 以下の要素は文のような形を成しているということに気づきます。つまり、(1) では＜主語 (a professional) ＋ 動詞 (paint)＞、(2) では＜主語 (the walls) ＋動詞 (painted)＞という具合です。(3) と (5) を比べると、(3) の動詞は原形であるのに対し、(5) の動詞は過去形になっており、文は時制を伴うということがわかります。(4) と (6) を比べると、どうでしょうか。(4) が (3) の受動文であるとすると、be 動詞が足りません。興味深いことに、make 使役と have 使役の場合は be 動詞は省略されてしまうのですが、let 使役動詞の場合は、be 動詞が省略されないので、≪使役動詞 ＋ 目的語 ＋ be 動詞 (原形) ＋ 過去分詞≫という形になります。let 使

役に倣って、(4) に be 動詞を加えますと、(7) のようになります。

　　(7) the walls be painted (by a professional)

では (7) と (6) を比較してみましょう。(7) の動詞は be 動詞の原形 be です。(6) の動詞は be 動詞の過去形 were です。つまり、こちらも動詞が時制を伴っているか否かという違いであることがわかります。以下に使役文の作り方を図解します。(8) は (1) の文、(9) は (2) の文の作り方です。

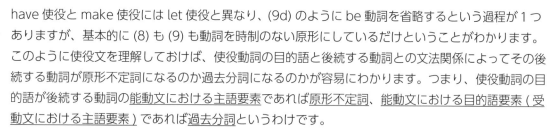

have 使役と make 使役には let 使役と異なり、(9d) のように be 動詞を省略するという過程が 1 つありますが、基本的に (8) も (9) も動詞を時制のない原形にしているだけということがわかります。このように使役文を理解しておけば、使役動詞の目的語と後続する動詞との文法関係によってその後続する動詞が原形不定詞になるのか過去分詞になるのかが容易にわかります。つまり、使役動詞の目的語が後続する動詞の<u>能動文における主語要素</u>であれば<u>原形不定詞</u>、<u>能動文における目的語要素（受動文における主語要素）</u>であれば<u>過去分詞</u>というわけです。

　しかしながら学習者の中には、原形不定詞を取るのか過去分詞を取るのかを《使役動詞 + 目的語（人）+ 原形不定詞》、《使役動詞 + 目的語（物）+ 過去分詞》と誤って記憶している人もいるのではないでしょうか。確かに使用頻度としては、目的語が人の時に原形不定詞、物の時に過去分詞というパターンが多いことは事実です。しかし、それはあくまでも一般化であり、そのようなパターンが規則として存在しているわけではありません。上述の通り、<u>原形不定詞になるのか過去分詞になるのかは、使役動詞に後続する文が能動文か受動文かというだけの違い</u>であるため、能動文の時でも目的語が人である場合もあれば、物である場合もあり、また受動文の時でも同じことが起こりうることになります。

では最後に使役動詞 make, have, let の使い方を確認しましょう。

使役動詞	例文
make	This song **made me cry**. Hillary Clinton **made it known** that she would run for the presidency.
have	She **had her bodyguards throw** her ex-husband out. I must **have my car checked** by the mechanic.
let	My parents never **let me drive** their car. The Prime Minister has **let it be known** that he has no intention of resigning. ＊使役動詞 let の場合、過去分詞の前の be を省略しないことに注意。

● Grammar Check

必要な場合は（　　　）内の動詞を適切な形にして文を完成させましょう。

1. Richard had his secretary _____ there alone. (go)

2. Anna inadvertently let the flowers _____. (droop)

3. I finally made myself _____ the room. (clean)

4. I am going to have the man _____. (charge)

5. Motherhood made me _____ how precious life is. (realize)

6. Ken managed to make himself _____ in Russian. (understand)

7. I'll have you _____ that she was given a full scholarship to Harvard University! (know)

8. We agree to let the car _____ on university property for an hour. (park)

Unit 3
ヴォーグへの道

◇ 本章スクリプト→ P. 85〜91　　DVD　Ch. 3　00:17:15-00:27:26

生まれ育ったロンドンの文化や父親のことをはじめ、アナは自らの生い立ちを語ります。アナの右腕であるグレイスも、熱心な『VOGUE』の読者だったと話します。二人が『VOGUE』の製作に関わるようになったきっかけとは……？

Communication Tip　　自然な会話術——"like"の様々な使い方

Warming Up
映画を視聴する前に確認しておきましょう

● **Vocabulary Check** Audio Track 8

映画の場面に出てくる語句を使って、空欄を埋めましょう。必要な場合は語形を変えてください。

- upbringing
- emancipation
- well-spoken
- fund
- components
- stylist
- stunning
- snapped

1. Sarah is a _____ student who gives clear and easy-to-follow oral presentations.
2. Please donate to help _____ research to find a cure for cancer.
3. The bride wore a _____ off-the-shoulder, fairy-tale wedding gown.
4. Tree branches _____ off along several streets due to the rain storm with high winds.
5. It is important to know that all _____ of physical fitness can be improved.
6. Her _____ largely influenced her decision to become a fashion designer.
7. Focusing largely on _____ , the politician campaigned for women's rights, liberation, and equality.
8. A _____ creates the looks that end up on the pages of fashion magazines.

Viewing

場面を視聴して内容をつかみましょう

● Comprehension

次の問題の答えを選択肢から選びなさい。正解を示す場面を見て確認してみましょう。

1. `DVD` `00:20:54-00:21:01`

While looking at Thakoon's sketches in Anna's office, Anna asks, "You like this one?" and Tonne, *Vogue*'s fashion director, replies, "I wouldn't discount that." What does Tonne's statement mean?

(A) Tonne believes the price of the clothing should not be lowered.
(B) Tonne would not dismiss or reject this clothing.
(C) Tonne does not want this clothing in a discount store.
(D) none of the above

2. `DVD` `00:21:17-00:21:26`

Sally, discussing *Vogue*'s fashion fund for new talent, says, "Remember Isaac Mizrahi went out of business. The fashion business isn't fair. They do everything right, and they still crash." The phrase <u>out of business</u> is closest in meaning to which other word or expression in Sally's quote?

(A) isn't fair
(B) do everything right
(C) crash
(D) all of the above

3. `DVD` `00:22:33-00:23:20`

True or false: Grace began her career at *Vogue* as a fashion model.

(A) true
(B) false

4. `DVD` `00:26:04-00:27:22`

What is the best way to describe Anna's feelings about the texture shoot photos?

(A) Anna wants to keep a certain photo because she's very interested in it.
(B) Anna wants to keep a certain photo because it makes her feel angry.
(C) Anna wants to take out a photo because it's very strange.
(D) Anna wants to take out a photo because she's not very interested in it.

• Dictation

音声を聞いて、シナリオの空所に当てはまる英語を書き入れましょう。

① 📀 00:20:41-00:21:26

Start ▶▶▶   ▶▶▶ End

Notes

Sally: It's very hard to be a 1. _____ in this country. So we created a fashion fund to draw attention to new 2. _____ , to fund it, and to . . . and to get mentoring for it. The winners get to design something for a mega-brand.

mentoring: 新入社員教育

Anna: You like this one?

Tonne: I wouldn't discount that. It's got a simplicity that the Gap 3. _____ is going to immediately acknowledge.

Sally: Thakoon was one of the winners of the award. He has all the 4. _____ to have a serious high-end designer line.

Anna: I'm happy with those three. Perfect. All right. Well, thank you.

Thakoon: Thank you.

Sally: You never know, though. I mean, remember Isaac Mizrahi went out of business. The fashion 5. _____ isn't fair. They do everything right, and they still crash.

Isaac Mizrahi: アイザック・ミズラヒ(アメリカの実力派ファッションデザイナー)

② 00:25:31-00:26:02 Audio Track 10

Sally: Grace is without question the greatest living 6. _____ . There's no one better than Grace. There's no one who can make any 7. _____ take more beautiful, more interesting, more romantic, more just 8. _____ realized pictures than Grace. There . . . there abso . . . there's no one better. Period. She comes from the idea that fashion is this world of play and 9. _____-_____ . It's . . . it's . . . as if someone's gone to the 10. _____-_____ box and found the most kind of wonderful, personal things, and put them together, but it's beautiful.

Post-Viewing: Review
発展演習で理解を深めましょう

• Discussion

ペアやグループで意見を交換しましょう。

1. Anna recalls how she got into the fashion industry when she says, "I think my father really decided for me that I should work in fashion." Who has influenced you in making decisions in your life? How did these people influence you?
2. Thakoon, designer and *Vogue* fashion fund recipient, remembers the day he met Anna. He says, "It's, like, Madonna is Anna." What does this comment mean? Think of other Madonnas in other industries such as arts, science, technology, or social media, and explain what they have done in their particular field.
3. Grace explains her first encounters with *Vogue* when she was a teenager in northern Wales. She says that what she saw in *Vogue* was "so entirely out of context compared to the lifestyle I led." Think of situations where you have felt "out of context" or different. What was so different for you?

Communication Tip

自然な会話術――"like"の様々な使い方

辞書を引くと、"like"には様々な意味があることがわかります。ここでは「～が好きだ」という意味の動詞ではなく、「～のようだ」のように前置詞や接続詞として使われる"like"について考えてみます。この映画でのタクーンの台詞に見られるように、"like"には4つの異なるくだけた口語的用法があります。これらは、1980年代のValley Girlと呼ばれる人たちが使ったことで有名になったものです。Valley Girlの言葉は、南カリフォルニアのSan Fernando Valleyのティーネイジャーのくだけた会話です。アメリカのロック・ミュージシャン、フランク・ザッパが1982年に発表した"Valley Girl"という歌に典型的に表れています。言語学者マーク・ヘイルによれば、若者が"like"という言葉を使うのは自らのアイデンティティーを表すものとして機能しています。つまり、この言葉を使うことで、自分が特定の世代に属していることを示しているというのです。

タクーンがタクシーの車内でアナとの最初の出会いについて語るとき、"like"がどう使われているか考えてみましょう。

> And I was just—She's like[1], 'Okay, go on.' So I'm, like[2], talking about the inspiration. Like[3], I'm moving my hands, and I'm, like[2], showing her, you know, the pieces. And I can see my hand, like[2], shaking. It was, like[2], shaking. Because she just sat there the whole time, like[4], 'Mm-hmm, mm-hmm.' So then we, we get out of there, and Meredith's like[1], 'Oh, my God, you were so well-spoken, but that hand kept shaking.'

(1) 最初の用法は"like[1]"と標記したもので、動詞sayの代わりに「be動詞 + like」を使って、実際に言った言葉か、それに近い言葉を続けるというものです。これはしばしば「引用のlike」("quotative like")と呼ばれ、アメリカ合衆国の25歳未満の人によく見られます。以下の例も見てみましょう。

- She's like[1], 'Okay, go on.'
- So then we, we get out of there, and Meredith's like[1], 'Oh, my God, you were so well-spoken, but that hand kept shaking'.

(2) 2番目の用法は"like[2]"と標記したもので、1950年代からアメリカのスラングになっているものです。この場合、"like"は間投詞（日本語で言う「えー」「あっ」など）のように使われます。強調したい時にも、明言を避けたい時にも使われます。以下の例も見てみましょう。

- So I'm, like[2], talking about the inspiration.
- And I can see my hand, like[2], shaking.

(3) 3番目の用法は"like[3]"と標記したもので、例示する時に使われます。この意味の"like"は、ふつう文頭におかれて、その前に言ったことの例をこれから挙げますよというシグナルになります。以下の例も見てみましょう。

... talking about the inspiration. Like[3], I'm moving my hands ...

(4) 4番目の用法は"like[(4)]"と標記したものです。"like"の後には単語を続けて「〜のような」という意味になるわけですが、その単語の代わりに擬音語や擬態語を続けるものです。驚いた時には"huh"を続けたり、痛みを覚えた時には"ouch"を続けたりします。この映画では一例出てきます。

Because she just sat there the whole time, like[(4)], 'Mm-hmm, mm-hmm.'

● Task

以下に映画のスクリプトの一部をあげます。適切な箇所に、上の4種類の"like"を入れてみましょう。口語表現の"like"が使いこなせるように、ペアで練習してください。

I think my father really decided for me that I should work in fashion. I can't remember what form it was I had to fill out. Maybe it was an admissions thing, and at the bottom, it said 'Career objectives,' you know, and I looked at it and said, 'What shall I do? How shall I fill this out?'

Unit 4
タクーン

◇ 本章スクリプト→ P. 92 〜 97　　DVD　Ch. 4　00:27:27-00:36:15

新進気鋭のデザイナーであるタクーンは特集企画のために服を製作中。一方、「ランスルー」で 9 月号に載せる服を吟味するアナ。その厳しい判断から "Ice woman" とも評される彼女ですが、そんなアナの娘ビーは母親やファッションの仕事をどう思っているのでしょうか。

Culture	写真家ブラッサイ	

Warming Up
映画を視聴する前に確認しておきましょう

● Vocabulary Check Audio Track 11

映画の場面に出てくる語句を使って、空欄を埋めましょう。必要な場合は語形を変えてください。

```
• exciting     • slash         • stubborn    • inspired
• evoke        • controversial • bored
```

1. She is a very ＿＿＿＿＿＿ girl; she will not change her mind once she has decided on something.

2. The dream I saw last night ＿＿＿＿＿＿ a happy time of my childhood.

3. Many companies ＿＿＿＿＿＿ off the product prices to win the competition.

4. A professor tried to find a ＿＿＿＿＿＿ topic for discussion in class.

5. Quotations of famous people from the past ＿＿＿＿＿＿ our daily lives.

6. At first, I wasn't interested in the film you showed me yesterday, but then it turned out to be ＿＿＿＿＿＿ .

7. Because children did not understand what the teacher said, they soon got ＿＿＿＿＿＿ .

Viewing
場面を視聴して内容をつかみましょう

● Comprehension

次の問題の答えを選択肢から選びなさい。正解を示す場面を見て確認してみましょう。

1. **DVD** | 00:28:23-00:28:40 |
   "Grace is very good at that," says Anna, "Go on, Grace. Slash and burn." The expression <u>slash and burn</u> is closest in meaning to
   (A) Cut some pictures in pieces and set them on fire.
   (B) Edit them down to a certain amount and use them in a different issue.
   (C) Say something ill about the pieces so that they can reduce the number of items.
   (D) Get rid of some of the fashion pieces that are not relevant for the issue.

2. **DVD** | 00:28:42-00:29:03 |
   Why does Anna introduce Thakoon while talking with Oscar?
   (A) She is going to ask Thakoon to "slash and burn" the pieces.
   (B) She would like to recommend him for Mango.
   (C) She would like to introduce him to Oscar.
   (D) Because Thakoon has started working for Anna.

3. **DVD** | 00:33:15-00:33:55 |
   In response to Anna's hard slashes of the run-through, Grace says, "Oh, please." In this context, the phrase <u>Oh, please</u> indicates
   (A) Grace's anger towards Anna makes a lot of clothes to be out of the way.
   (B) that Grace is fed up with Anna's suggestion towards fur clothing.
   (C) that Grace is asking Virginia to find a fur hat to match the fur coat.
   (D) Grace's depression her ideas are turned down by Anna.

4. **DVD** | 00:34:12-00:34:22 |
   Why was the cover of one of the past September issues controversial?
   (A) Because Anna put a black girl on the September cover.
   (B) Because a cover model wore fur on the September issue.
   (C) Because the cover model looked pale.
   (D) Because Anna used a celebrity as a cover girl.

5. **DVD** | 00:35:20-00:36:12 |
   What is the main reason that Bee (Anna Wintour's daughter) chooses not to work in the fashion industry?
   (A) She does not want her mother to push her to be the second "Anna Wintour".
   (B) She wants to be a lawyer.
   (C) She does not like *Vogue* magazine.
   (D) She thinks fashion is not the career she wants to follow.

● Dictation

音声を聞いて、シナリオの空所に当てはまる英語を書き入れましょう。

① 📀 00:29:49-00:30:32   🔊 Audio Track 12

Notes

Grace: I moved on. I'm onto twenties now. Twenties is something that . . . Well, really the inspiration was John Galliano's show. He was 1. _____ by the photographer Brassaï, who was a photographer from the twenties. Shoes, I'm very 2. _____ _____ . It just has to be something that 3. _____ evokes the twenties. What has she got? Well. You have to have that fashion story, you know, spots are in or stripes or full skirts or straight skirts or whatever it is. But I've tried to make that 4. _____ . We build a fantasy around the girl and what she's doing, what she's thinking, who she is.

evoke: 呼び起こす、喚起する

② 📀 00:31:09-00:31:55   🔊 Audio Track 13

Grace: I have a ton of stuff here, and I don't know how many doubles, triples, singles I'm doing.
Anna: But maybe we can prioritize.
Grace: But, yeah. and you should, you know, if you hate something, just say "I never want to see that in the magazine."

Anna: Okay.

Grace: Oh . . . there's two coats here. I'm . . . I'm sort of 5. _____ about them. But I'm trying . . .

Anna: It is 6. _____ _____ the one we did in July.

Grace: It's not because you're thinking of the one we shot and 7. _____ _____ . I've shot them twice, but we have not had them in the magazine. The coat didn't run. Anyway, there's all these little dresses. And then there's a little coat. I love all these little evening things.

Anna: Let's remove the coat.

Grace: I . . . I have to have a little freedom to 8. _____ _____ .

Anna: Grace . . . I mean, there's a lot of 9. _____ things in this, and I want this to be more 9. _____ than not.

Post-Viewing: Review
発展演習で理解を深めましょう

● Discussion

ペアやグループで意見を交換しましょう。

1. Grace describes herself and Anna as "stubborn". In which scene can you see that? And when you have to work with stubborn people, how do you cope with them?
2. When Anna and Bee talk about past *Vogue* covers, they state that the cover with a black girl was "controversial". Do you think it is controversial? Why?
3. If you were Anna's daughter, would you like to be an editor like her? Why?

Culture
写真家ブラッサイ

Grace: I moved on. I'm onto twenties now. Twenties is something that . . . Well, really the inspiration was John Galliano's show. He was inspired by the photographer Brassaï, who was a photographer from the twenties.

　グレイスの台詞の中に出てくる Brassaï。彼は 1899 年生まれで、20 世紀に活躍した写真家です。ハンガリー（現ルーマニア）出身であり、名前の Brassaï は彼が生まれた町 "Brasso" から付けた彼のペンネームのようなもので、本名は Gyula Halász（ジュラ・ハラーシュ）というそうです。もともとは画家を目指してブタペストの美術学校にて学び、その後ベルリンにて美術の勉強を続けますが、1924 年にフランス・パリに移住してジャーナリストとなります。ジャーナリストとして写真術を覚えた Brassaï は、以後、写真を撮り始めます。

　パリの裏側に魅せられて写真家へと転身し、パリを拠点として活動しました。1933 年には『夜のパリ』と題した初写真集を、1976 年には『未知のパリ・深夜のパリ』という写真集を出版しています。これは 1930 年代の夜のパリを歩き回りながら、特にパリの裏社会（娼婦や裏路地の人やもの）や大衆文化などに焦点を当てた写真を集め、Brassaï 自身が文章を添えたものです。アヘン窟でアヘンを吸う人々の写真など、かなり際どい写真も紹介されています。

　グレイスが映画の中で、9 月号の撮影のテーマを話し合っているときに見ていた写真集が、この『未知のパリ・深夜のパリ』（*Le Paris Secret des Années 30*）です。グレイスが "She has big, fat legs and things. I love that." と言っていた写真は "La Môme Bijou"（飯島耕一訳では「宝石の女」）という写真で、1932 年に撮られたものです。

　他にも Brassaï は当時のシュルレアリスムの作家などと交流があり、『作家の誕生──ヘンリー・ミラー』や『語るピカソ』など、芸術家たちとの交流を独特の語り口でつづった著書も出版しています。また自身もシュルレアリスムの写真家と呼ばれることもあったようです。

　アメリカの批評家スーザン・ソンタグは著書 *On Photography* においてシュルレアリスムにおける写真について、以下のように述べています。

① 日本語に訳してみましょう。

The arts in which Surrealism has come into its own are prose fiction (as content, mainly, but much more abundant and more complex thematically than that claimed by painting), theatre, the arts of assemblage, and—most triumphantly—photography. That photography is the only art that is natively surreal does not mean, however, that it shares the destinies of the official Surrealist movement.

Notes　prose fiction: 散文（定型にこだわらない通常の文章）　assemblage: アッサンブラージュ芸術
triumphantly: 勝ち誇って、高らかに

ソンタグはこの本の中で、写真が「中流階級のフラネール（ぶらぶら歩く人）の眼の延長」として機能し、写真家たちは「都会の表向きの現実ではなく、その暗い裏側の隅」に惹かれると書いています。その中には、Brassaï の名も挙がっています。
　「花の街」と呼ばれるファッショナブルで優美なイメージがあるパリの裏側を多く写真に収めたことを考えると、Brassaï がシュルレアリスムの写真家として分類されることも納得がいきますね。
　またソンタグは同書の中で、Brassaï について次のように言っています。

② 日本語に訳してみましょう。
　Brassaï denounced photographers who try to trap their subjects off-guard, in the erroneous belief that something special will be revealed about them.
　　Notes　off-guard: 不意に、油断して　erroneous: 間違った

● **Research Activities**

シュルレアリスムとはどんな作風のものを指すのでしょう？　そして、どんな作家や画家、写真家などが含まれるのでしょう？

Unit 5
締め切りまで6週間

◇ 本章スクリプト→ P. 98 ～ 105   DVD Ch. 5   00:36:16-00:46:14

締め切り6週間前。9月号で特集するモデルの写真撮影が本格的に始まります。それぞれの特集で撮影された写真の候補から、アナが掲載写真の取捨選択をします。グレイスは趣向を凝らし、自信作とも言える出来映えの写真を数多く用意するのですが……。

Grammar　　等位接続詞（coordinating conjunctions）

Warming Up
映画を視聴する前に確認しておきましょう

● Vocabulary Check   🔊 Audio Track 14

映画の場面に出てくる語句を使って、空欄を埋めましょう。必要な場合は語形を変えてください。

| • fabulous | • upside down | • fade | • rework |
| • inspiration | • run-through | • ahead of the curve | • appreciate |

1. There is much confusion regarding the difference between _____ and repair in a manufacturing environment.
2. Why do Special Forces personnel wear their wristwatches _____?
3. It would be really _____ if you could complete the questionnaire.
4. This bracelet when first polished looks very glorious, but time makes it _____ , and turn to a pale yellow.
5. I'll look everything over and if we need a second _____ it won't take too long.
6. Taking _____ from both modern and historical fashion can be a great way to infuse something new and fresh in your designs.
7. The laboratory acquired a _____ reputation for its historic discovery.
8. The American version of *Vogue* has stayed _____ in the fashion industry since Anna has been at the helm.

Viewing
場面を視聴して内容をつかみましょう

• Comprehension

次の問題の答えを選択肢から選びなさい。正解を示す場面を見て確認してみましょう。

1. 📀 `00:39:09-00:39:23`

When Thakoon is talking with a woman at the party, he says, "It's sick." Which phrase is the closest in meaning to <u>It's sick</u>?

(A) I feel awful.
(B) It's horrible.
(C) It's cool.
(D) I feel sick.

2. 📀 `00:37:55-00:38:28`

Grace is telling Charlie that the pictures are meant to be soft because

(A) she wants them to look fake.
(B) she wants them to be pumped up.
(C) she wants them to be pin-sharp.
(D) she wants them to be like old film.

> **Notes**　pin-sharp: 極めて鮮明な

3. 📀 `00:45:16-00:45:27`

Laurie expresses her opinion about Grace's pictures. How does Grace feel about Laurie's response?

(A) She is so glad that Laurie likes Galliano.
(B) She is very pleased to hear that Laurie agrees to tell her opinion to Anna.
(C) She is quite happy and she wants Laurie to mention her opinion to Anna.
(D) She is very mad at Laurie because it is too late to put them back.

4. 📀 `00:45:57-00:46:10`

What does Tonne mean by "this is gonna be highly produced"?

(A) It is costly to shoot a weekend in Rome.
(B) A lot of pictures will be shot in a short period of time.
(C) They are planning to produce a new trend in the fashion industry.
(D) A lot of storyboards will be prepared for Sienna.

• Dictation

音声を聞いて、シナリオの空所に当てはまる英語を書き入れましょう。

① DVD 00:37:49-00:38:29   Audio Track 15

Start ▶▶▶   ▶▶▶ End

Grace: The girls were 1. _____ , and . . . uh . . . they all seemed to work perfectly. I . . . I hope it looks as good as I think it does. We've done them in a very soft color. You know, it's almost like old film that's 2. _____ . I love when . . . when it goes soft and even sometimes if there's 3. _____ , there's a little blur and things, but . . . I don't know. Everybody seems to like things 4. _____ these days. I think it's a 5. _____ .

② DVD 00:44:21-00:45:14   Audio Track 16

Start ▶▶▶   ▶▶▶ End

Tonne: The 6. _____ for *Vogue* to putting celebrities on its covers has been because of Anna. She was 7. _____ _____ _____ _____ to appreciate the fact that celebrity culture became overwhelming.

Sienna: 8. _____ _____ _____ _____ pose in this bit?

Tonne: No, darling.

Sienna: I don't know.

Sally: What *Vogue* did and what the supermodels did in the pages of *Vogue* is that they trained a generation of celebrities to want to be supermodels. Actresses 9._____ _____ that fashion was a seamless part of life and a seamless part of celebrity, and that was fine.

Anna: [*Gasps, chuckles*]

Woman: Oh, my goodness.

Sienna: It's amazing. Really, no pasta. I can't bear going to Rome and not being able to have pasta. That's incredible.

Anna: It is. You 10._____ _____ in that.

Post-Viewing: Review
発展演習で理解を深めましょう

● Discussion

ペアやグループで意見を交換しましょう。

1. Anna puts aside the picture that Grace thinks is the best. Anna's point of view and Grace's are totally incompatible. It seems that the Design Director Charlie acts as a mediator between them. If you were Charlie, what would you do?
2. Sienna says, "Really, no pasta. I can't bear going to Rome and not being able to have pasta." Why does she say that?
3. Suppose you are working for a company where your boss is very powerful like Anna. Your proposal may be rejected. How would you convince your boss to adopt your idea?

Grammar
等位接続詞 (coordinating conjunctions)

Sienna: I can't bear going to Rome and not being able to have pasta.

　接続詞には大きく分けて、等位接続詞 (coordinating conjunctions) と従位接続詞 (subordinate conjunctions) があります。等位接続詞はその名の通り、接続する 2 つの要素を等位に接続します。文法上対等の関係にある要素を繋ぐことができる接続詞なので、必ず語と語、句と句、節と節の組み合わせになります。また語と語の場合も名詞と名詞、動詞と動詞、句と句の場合も名詞句と名詞句、動詞句と動詞句というように同じ仲間同士で接続します。従位接続詞は従節を主節に結びつける接続詞なので繋ぐ要素は節と節に限られます。ここでは等位接続詞について考えてみましょう。

　ではまずは上のシエナ・ミラーの台詞に出てきた等位接続詞 and を例に考えましょう。この and は何と何を繋いでいるのでしょうか。この and に後続する部分を見ますと、not being able to have pasta とあります。否定の not は肯定・否定を表すマーカーのようなものなので、それを除いた部分を見てみます。すると being able to have pasta という動名詞句になっていることに気づきます。では and の前はどうなっているでしょうか。やはりこちらも going to Rome という動名詞句があることに気づきます。つまり、ここで and が接続しているのは going to Rome と not being able to have pasta という動名詞句であることがわかります。よってこの文の意味は「ローマに行ってパスタが食べられない」のは I can't bear「耐えられない」となるのです。

● Grammar Check

等位接続されている語・句・節に誤りがある場合はそれを正し、文を完成させましょう。また文が正しい場合は問題番号を○で囲みましょう。

1. Mary held her baby more tightly and begins to sing again.

2. They are capable not only of knowing but also to preserve their knowledge.

3. Either the manager or his assistant made the request.

4. John practices the guitar every day and playing well.

5. Can't you see how fool and crazy this statement is?

6. He often sends contributions to that newspaper, but they are written by his wife.

7. I don't like typing and to proofread my own papers.

8. Our company is dedicated to product quality and satisfy customer.

Unit 6

パリへ

◇ 本章スクリプト→P. 106〜109　　DVD Ch. 6　　00:46:16-00:53:30

撮影や打ち合わせのため、ローマやパリなど、ヨーロッパ各地へ旅立つスタッフたち。グレイスは、予算をかけこだわりを尽くした自分の特集が報われず不機嫌な様子で、カメラの前でぼやきます。そんな彼女もアナに同行し、パリへと出発します。

Communication Tip　　自然な会話術──"Hi" と "Hello" だけではない会話中のあいさつ表現

Warming Up
映画を視聴する前に確認しておきましょう

● Vocabulary Check Audio Track 17

映画の場面に出てくる語句を使って、空欄を埋めましょう。必要な場合は語形を変えてください。

```
• itinerary    • budget    • wig        • lackluster
• whittle down • worth     • collection
```

1. Universities are challenged with the idea that _____ web design is turning off prospective students.
2. The new dress _____ is described as focusing on "creativity, fun, and love of fashion."
3. The detailed travel _____ includes five countries in Europe.
4. A month's _____ of rain is expected to fall over a period of only a few days.
5. The original 42 entries were _____ to 11 official contestants.
6. The donated hair and money will be used to produce _____ for cancer patients.
7. Students are holding a protest about _____ cuts which will impact the purchase of classroom supplies.

Viewing

場面を視聴して内容をつかみましょう

● Comprehension

次の問題の答えを選択肢から選びなさい。正解を示す場面を見て確認してみましょう。

1. *DVD* `00:48:03-00:48:21`

Grace says, "I'm in a really foul mood because they've killed a lot of the spread of my twenties story." What does "kill" mean in this context?

(A) to cancel
(B) to take out
(C) to do away with
(D) all of the above

2. *DVD* `00:48:21-00:48:33`

True or false: Grace is embarrassed to talk about money and the budget in front of the camera crew.

(A) true
(B) false

3. *DVD* `00:49:09-00:49:27`

Why will the cover model, Sienna Miller, wear a wig for the photo shoot?

(A) Her hair is too short.
(B) Her hair is not lackluster enough.
(C) She's growing her hair out and refuses to have it cut.
(D) She wants to cut her hair.

> **Notes** lackluster: つやがない

4. *DVD* `00:47:17-00:53:32`

Put the following events in the order in which they occur in the film by writing 1-4 on the lines below. (1 = first, 4 = last)

_____ (A) Anna leaves for Europe.
_____ (B) Jean Paul Gaultier shows Anna a new dress which will be part of a collection of different princes of different countries.
_____ (C) Grace is upset about her photos being taken out of the magazine.
__1__ (D) Anna and Grace discuss the budget.

● Dictation

音声を聞いて、シナリオの空所に当てはまる英語を書き入れましょう。

① 📀 00:47:25-00:48:33 🔊 Audio Track 18

Anna: Grace, I'm leaving soon. Do you need me for anything?

Grace: Umm . . . Well, yeah, we have, uh . . . you know, like . . . Are there any restrictions on the Couture? The 1. _____ is a problem, because, you know—

Anna: Christiane says the budget is fine.

Grace: It's not fine. It's not fine. It's not that simple.

Anna: This is . . . Well, you need to talk with her because she has the 2. _____ .

Grace: I know, but it's a hell of a lot of work to put together, which I don't want to do if you have a 3. _____ budget. So I can't really find out what the limit is . . . 'cause the limit keeps changing.

Now, I'm in a really 4. _____ mood because they've killed a lot of the spread of my twenties story. And they're about to kill another one. And they're all lying to me about it, including Danko, who I thought was my friend. You just sit here and everything is killed. It's, like, incredibly 5. _____ . And I love to talk money in front of you guys with Anna . . . 'cause it drives her crazy. [*laughs*] It's a sure way to get the budget up.

a hell of: [形＋名の前に置いて] とても、どえらい

drive someone crazy: …をいらいらさせる

② **Start ▶▶▶**  **▶▶▶ End**

Grace: Well, no, you're taking them all down. You're taking everything down. They took two more out, and there's 6. _____ marks on two more. So it's been 7. _____ _____ and I'm furious. They've probably thrown out $50,000 8. _____ of work. I care very much about what I do. I do, or I 9. _____ be still doing it, you know. Um . . . But it gets harder and harder to see it just 10. _____ out. [*pause*] And it's very hard to go onto the next thing.

Post-Viewing: Review
発展演習で理解を深めましょう

● Discussion

ペアやグループで意見を交換しましょう。

1. Fashion magazines, like *Vogue*, have budgets for their photo shoots. In other words, there is a certain amount of money they can spend to create a photo spread in the magazine. What kind of a personal budget do you have? What things must you budget for and what things would you like to buy for fun?
2. A large part of Anna's job as editor is to decide what stays in the magazine. As part of this process, she has to whittle down photo shoots as seen when she says to Charles (fashion director), "This . . . this [photo spread] is too long, Charlie." Was there a time in your life when you had to make a difficult decision? How did you go about making it?
3. Anna meets Jean Paul Gaultier, a French haute couture fashion designer, in Paris where he shows her some new designs. If you could design a new outfit, what would it include, and why?

Communication Tip

自然な会話術——"Hi" と "Hello" だけではない会話中のあいさつ表現

　あいさつは会話における重要な要素です。あいさつは、子供が最初に習得する発話行為であり、外国語の授業の最初のレッスンで習うでしょう。あいさつは相手に注意を喚起したり、相互対話の場を築いたりします。次の会話文に見られるように、あいさつは組対話のひとつとなっています。つまり、話者Aが話者Bにあいさつをすれば、話者Bは受け答えをすることになっているのです。

　　A: Hello. How are you?
　　B: I'm fine, thank you. And you?
　　A: I'm fine too.

とはいえ、上記のような会話が起こることは現実にはまれです。人間は必ずしも教科書に書かれている対話文の通りにしゃべるわけではありません。学習者であるみなさんにとって難しいと感じるのは、「語用論的な能力」と呼ばれるような能力を理解し、使いこなすことでしょう。語用論的な能力というのは、ある特定の状況において、社会的・文化的な慣習に基づいて、ひとまとまりの発話がどのように使われ、理解されてきたかを意識できる能力のことです。こういった語用に気づくことによって、特定の状況で特定の語や熟語がどのように使われるかを理解することができるのです。こういった語用のルールをうまく守れるようになるために、ここでは会話におけるあいさつを学びましょう。
　インフォーマルかフォーマルか、気楽なのか真剣なのかといった状況に応じて、異なるタイプのあいさつを用いないといけません。この章で取り上げた場面でも、以下のようなあいさつが出てきます。

　　Tonne: Didier? I'm fine. How are you?

　　Anna:　How are you, Grace?
　　Anna:　Hi, how are you?

　　Jean Paul: How are you, Anna? Nice to see you.
　　Anna:　　Nice to see you, too.
　　Jean Paul: Pleasure to see you.

　『VOGUE』編集部は職場ですから、上記の例よりももっとフォーマルな言葉が使われているのではと考えてしまうかもしれませんが、職場でも、とりわけ長期間共に働いてきた同僚同士であれば、くだけた会話表現も使われます。つまり、どこで英語を使うかを考えて言葉を選ばないといけないのです。フォーマルな状況とは、先生、上司、同僚、客、見知らぬ人などと話をするときです。インフォーマルな状況とは、家族、友人、クラスメートと話をするようなときです。

● Task 1

下の表は、アメリカでの一般的なあいさつ表現の例です。左の列にあいさつの意味を英語で書いてください。右の列にその受け答えとして適切な英語を書いてください。1行目と真ん中の列はすでに埋めてありますので、それにならって穴埋めをしていくとよいでしょう。

Meaning	Greetings	Replies
Hello	Hello Hi Hey	*Hello; Hi; Hey; any of the greetings in this table*
	How are you? How are ya*? How are you doing? How's it going? How's everything? How are things? How's life?	
	What's up? What's new? What's going on?	
	Good to see you. Nice to see you.	
	Long time no see. It's been awhile.	

※ "ya" はインフォーマルな状況で使える "you" の短縮表現です。

驚くかもしれませんが、同じ列にあるあいさつ表現は交換して使っても問題ないのです。"How are you?" と言ったら "I'm fine, thank you" と答えるような、典型的な教科書通りの表現を超えて、異なる受け答えの練習をしてみましょう。

● Task 2

Task 1 の真ん中の列のあいさつ表現を取り上げ、下の表のフォーマルとインフォーマルに分けてみましょう。あいさつ表現の中には、フォーマルな状況でもインフォーマルな状況でも使えるものがあります。最初の表現だけはすでに振り分けていますので、これに続けて分けてみましょう。

Formal	Informal
Hello	*Hi*

言葉やその語用をより深く意識することで、もっと豊かで意義のある会話ができるようになるでしょう。

● Task 3

少人数のグループで、2つの短いダイアローグを作ってください。ひとつめのダイアローグはフォーマルな状況で、もうひとつはインフォーマルな状況でのダイアローグにしてください。そのダイアローグをクラスメートの前でやりとりしてみましょう。

Formal	Informal

Unit 7
パリ オートクチュール・コレクション

◆ 本章スクリプト→ P. 110～114　　DVD　Ch. 7　00:53:31-01:02:22

『VOGUE』に関わってから、グレイスは長年パリに縁があるようです。クチュール・コレクションを観たあと、アナは打ち合わせのためロンドンへ。パリとローマでは、新たに写真撮影が行われます。9月号の表紙を飾るシエナ・ミラーはどのように撮影されるのでしょう。

| Culture | 映画『ローマの休日』のアン王女の言葉遣い |

Warming Up
映画を視聴する前に確認しておきましょう

● Vocabulary Check　　　　　　　　　　　　　Audio Track 20

映画の場面に出てくる語句を使って、空欄を埋めましょう。必要な場合は語形を変えてください。

> - ostensibly　　- thrust　　- waste　　- incredible
> - charge　　- direction　　- convince

1. David visited Paris _____ for the international conference.
2. Because of mass consumption, a lot of natural resources are _____ .
3. Emily told me the right _____ to the bus stop.
4. She has _____ her boss to abolish the smoking area from the office.
5. Magic is not the _____ of the Harry Potter series.
6. He happened to make an _____ discovery while digging the Maya ruins.
7. Anna always _____ ahead to pursue new fashion scenes for *Vogue* magazine.

Viewing

場面を視聴して内容をつかみましょう

• Comprehension

次の問題の答えを選択肢から選びなさい。正解を示す場面を見て確認してみましょう。

1. 📀 `00:53:48-00:54:03`

Grace cites Anna's comment "Don't be silly. We can't do that one." What does Anna mean by this comment?

(A) The *Vogue* budget does not allow them to shoot in Paris.
(B) Grace is always inspired by too many things, so some of them cannot be used.
(C) Grace cannot do a shoot in Paris because Anna does not like to work in Paris.
(D) Anna thinks Grace is silly because she does not understand what Anna wants.

2. 📀 `00:55:21-00:55:53`

When Mario says, "I want to create a film", what does he really mean?

(A) He would like to shoot a film based on the *Vogue* models.
(B) The theme of the photo shoots is a moody Italian film.
(C) He has the cinematic theme for shoots in Rome in his mind.
(D) He likes to use the room for the shoot because it is amazing.

3. 📀 `00:56:20-00:56:45`

Anna says, "if we decide on a look and just stay with it". What is she talking about?

(A) She wants only one hair style for Sienna's shoot.
(B) She does not want Mario to try many locations using white.
(C) She wants Sienna to wear a blond wig because her hair is not good.
(D) She does not want to waste time, so she only wants one shot of Sienna.

4. 📀 `00:57:48-00:58:11`

Why doesn't Grace take a nap in the car?

(A) Because she was taught to keep watching as there are many inspirations around her.
(B) Grace feels tense during her trip, so she cannot sleep in the car.
(C) Because the sights in Paris are very beautiful and new to her.
(D) Grace wants to find the best place to have her shoot for the September issue.

5. 📀 `01:01:28-01:01:36`

Why doesn't Raquel (a model) eat pie until the end of her shoot?

(A) Grace stopped her, as she might drop it on the clothes she is wearing.
(B) Grace did not buy enough pies for all the staff members, so Raquel is not sure if she can eat one.
(C) Raquel cannot eat anything because the corset is too tight.
(D) Raquel thinks she might not fit in the corset after eating pie.

● **Dictation**

音声を聞いて、シナリオの空所に当てはまる英語を書き入れましょう。

① 00:57:31-00:59:25　　　Audio Track 21

Notes

Grace: Paris is so beautiful. It really is. I never 1. _____ to be a model or never, never dreamt to be a fashion editor. But I just loved the pages and the pictures. In my early years as a fashion editor, uh . . . I worked with Norman Parkinson, who was a really big 2. _____ . And he taught me to always keep your eyes open, you know, never go to sleep in the car or anything like that. Keep watching, because whatever you see out the window or wherever, it can 3. _____ you.

It is amazing. It's . . . it's sort of strange to think how old it is. It's beautiful. I think I got 4. _____ _____ somewhere, 'cause I'm, you know, still 5. _____ _____ . You have to go charging ahead. You can't stay behind.

Norman Parkinson:
ノーマン・パーキンソン（ファッションや人物写真の分野を代表するイギリスの写真家）

② 00:59:51-01:00:38　　　 Audio Track 22

Tonne: Anna? How are you? We're doing very well. I'm sitting here with Mario and everybody. Sienna's here. We're doing a wig. Everything's great.

Mario:	Let's 6. _____ our story like this. Let's do four visual locations. Let's say . . .
Tonne:	That's pretty 7. _____ , don't you think?
Mario:	Yeah.
Tonne:	I mean, look. You've got the Colosseum.
Mario:	It is beautiful.
Tonne:	It's beautiful.
Mario:	I think we don't need it.
Tonne:	It's got beautiful open- 8. _____ light. I mean, it's so pretty.
Mario:	That is what I'm wondering: whether we want pretty. I find I've done this hair, like, really—I would love something new. A new proposition.
Woman:	Yeah.
Tonne:	We tried the wig, and it did not work. And we 9. _____ _____ . And we moved on in the right 10. _____ , I think.

Colosseum: コロセウム（ローマの円形闘技場）

Post-Viewing: Review
発展演習で理解を深めましょう

● **Discussion**

ペアやグループで意見を交換しましょう。

1. When Anna and Mario talk about the cover shoot of the September issue in Rome, Mario says, "I want to create a film." If you were to do the shoot in Rome, where would you choose to go? What kind of story can you think of behind that shoot?
2. Grace states, "Keep watching, because whatever you see out the window or wherever, it can inspire you." What kinds of things inspire you in your daily life?
3. In the couture shoot, Grace bought some pies as a gift for Raquel and other staff. If you were Grace, what kind of gift would you bring for Raquel and staff? Why?

Culture
映画『ローマの休日』のアン王女の言葉遣い

　マリオとアナの会話の中で、*Roman Holiday*（『ローマの休日』）の話が出てきましたね。『ローマの休日』は1953年にアメリカで公開され、日本でも翌年1954年に公開された映画で、ラブ・コメディと位置づけされています。まだ名もなき女優だったオードリー・ヘップバーンがチャーミングなアン王女を演じ、一気にスターダムへと駆け上がるきっかけとなった映画です。この作品で、オードリーは当時24歳にしてアカデミー主演女優賞を受賞しました。

　トリニタ・デイ・モンティ教会の前のスペイン階段でジェラードを食べるシーンは日本では大変有名です（現在は、あの階段は飲食禁止だそうです。残念ですね）。

　それ以外にも、アン王女が街中を乗り回したスクーター、ヴェスパ（"Vespa"）は、当時大流行したそうです。ちなみにVespaというのはイタリア語でスズメバチを意味し、そのお尻の膨らんだフォルムがスズメバチに似ていることから名づけられているそうです。

　アン王女は重厚で厳格な造りの寝室を抜け出し、音楽や明るいことがあふれている「外」へと飛び出します。アン王女は「休日」を過ごす中で、髪を切り、街を歩き回り、お酒やタバコ、スクーターの運転など（どう見ても）初めてのことを経験していきます。そして初めての恋も。ヒステリーを起こして泣きじゃくっていたアン王女は消え失せ、彼女は自分の王女としての責任を思い出します。24時間後寝室へ戻ってきたアン王女は、まるで別人です。

　それでは、映画の最後にあるアン王女の会見を訳してみましょう。ここでも、「王女」への記者会見ということを踏まえた言葉遣いに気を付けましょう。

　王女が会場へ入場し、会見が始まります。王女は初恋の相手のJoe（記者）が来ていることに気づきますが、努めて平静をよそおいます。

　一人の記者が「ヨーロッパの経済問題は同盟により解決し得るとお考えですか？」と問いかけ、王女が答えます。

> **Ann:** I am in favour of any measure which would lead to closer cooperation in Europe.

　二人目の記者が、国家間の友好関係の前途について、王女の意見をたずねます。

> **Ann:** I have every faith in it . . . as I have faith in relations between people.

　そして王女は、最後の質問に、Joeを見つめて答えにつまります。

> **Correspondent 1:** Which of the cities visited did Your Highness enjoy the most?
> **General Provno:** Each, in its own way . . .
> **Ann:** Each, in its own way, was unforgettable . . . it would be difficult to

— Rome! By all means, Rome. I will cherish my visit here in memory as long as I live.

Correspondent 2: Despite your indisposition, Your Highness?

Ann: Despite that.

> **Notes**　Your Highness: 女王殿下

● Research Activities

　『ローマの休日』の舞台はローマですが、製作国はアメリカ合衆国です。この映画の脚本のクレジットは、公開当時は Ian McLellan Hunter となっていましたが、実際に脚本を書いたのは Dalton Trumbo でした。

　なぜ実際の脚本家ではない Hunter が「脚本家」としてクレジットされ、実際の脚本家がクレジットされなかったのか、当時のアメリカの歴史的背景を調べ、考察してみましょう。

Unit 8
テニスコートのアンドレ

◇ 本章スクリプト→ P. 115 〜 120　　DVD　Ch. 8　01:02:23-01:11:40

アンドレがテニスを始めたのには理由があるようです。そして締め切り1週間前。パリとローマで撮影された掲載候補の写真チェックが行われ、パリでの撮影を監督したグレイスが写真の仕上がりに満足する一方、ローマで撮影されたシエナの写真チェックでは一悶着がありそうです。

| **Grammar** | 動名詞と不定詞 |

Warming Up
映画を視聴する前に確認しておきましょう

● **Vocabulary Check**　　 Audio Track 23

映画の場面に出てくる語句を使って、空欄を埋めましょう。必要な場合は語形を変えてください。

```
• inaugurate    • aesthetics    • couture        • snatch
• hinge         • ravishing     • conservative   • restrain
```

1. _____ is the philosophical study of beauty and taste.

2. Haute _____ is the French word for high fashion.

3. Sienna Miller is _____ in a red cutout dress.

4. Many prestigious banks and small professional firms are still very _____ about clothing.

5. Disturbing video shows a young girl being _____ out of a store by a man.

6. I took a long breath and managed to _____ my anger.

7. Our show's success _____ on our ability to understand our exhibitors and attendees.

8. President Obama was _____ on January 20th, 2009.

Viewing

場面を視聴して内容をつかみましょう

● Comprehension

次の問題の答えを選択肢から選びなさい。正解を示す場面を見て確認してみましょう。

1. **DVD** `01:02:45-01:03:01`

   André says that Anna saved his life. What did Anna actually do to him?
   (A) She helped him when he was playing tennis three years ago.
   (B) She asked him to do something to lose weight.
   (C) She told him to go to tennis school.
   (D) She told him that there would be many interruptions in his work due to his weight issues.

2. **DVD** `01:05:10-01:08:22`

   Anna is so eager to see whether cover photographer Mario has taken a picture at the Colosseum or not. What is the problem?
   (A) It is important to know how many pictures he has taken in order to decide how many pages the September issue contains.
   (B) He doesn't take a picture because he doesn't want to do it.
   (C) She needs more pictures of clothes but he has sent fewer pictures than she has expected.
   (D) He does not send all the film at once and the rest is upon request.

3. **DVD** `01:08:25-01:08:50`

   Anna talks with a lady named Florence at Bee's house. What is Florence likely to do?
   (A) She is a secretary of Anna.
   (B) She is a judge.
   (C) She is a home helper.
   (D) She is a lawyer.

4. **DVD** `01:08:50-01:09:39`

   Which statement is true about Anna's family?
   (A) Her two brothers and her sister are not interested in what Anna is currently doing.
   (B) Her older brother is a fund manager in London.
   (C) Her sister is supporting farmers in South America.
   (D) Her younger brother is an editor of a newspaper.

● Dictation

音声を聞いて、シナリオの空所に当てはまる英語を書き入れましょう。

① 01:07:17-01:08:08　　　　　Audio Track 24

Start ▶▶▶　　　**▶▶▶ End**

 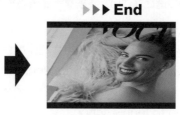

Notes

Charlie: I just finished 1. _____ to Mario.
Tonne: Yeah.
Charlie: He says there is nothing on the dress at the Colosseum.
Tonne: Well, he didn't like it. He really couldn't.
Charlie: He says he didn't like it, so he never really did it, he said . . .
Tonne: But, he . . .
Charlie: . . . which I had to tell her.
Tonne: He . . . You know, it's digital.
Charlie: I know.
Tonne: He did something, but he never got an image that he wanted 2. _____ _____ _____ .
Charlie: Right.
Tonne: You know, I understand that, you know, she needs a few more dresses but, you know, you get what you get.
Charlie: I'm concerned a little 'cause I'm not 3. _____ _____ _____ the cover at the moment. The one he's chosen, she's kind of tough-looking in the face.

tough-looking: こわもてな、厳しそうな

Tonne: Right.
Charlie: That's not a face for a cover.
Tonne: Right.
Charlie: See this.
Tonne: Yeah. I mean . . .
Charlie: This . . . It can't be that.
Tonne: I mean, I think there could be 4. _____ be something there.
Charlie: That's what I think.
Tonne: So I . . . I think that's pretty 5. _____ .
Charlie: Well. Look at it now. I've cropped in on it and turned it.

Tonne: What does it say? Something.
Charlie: [*sighs*] And . . .
Tonne: 'Like this best, but teeth.'
Charlie: 'But teeth.'

② 📀 01:11:13–01:11:39

Start ▶▶▶   ▶▶▶ **End**

Anna: I remember when my dad 6. _____ , and I asked him why he was leaving because he was obviously so 7. _____ _____ what he was doing still. And he said, 'Well, I get too angry. I get too angry and I 8. _____ _____ _____ too angry.' So I do remember that, because I know there are times I get quite angry. So I try and 9. _____ that. So I think when I 8. _____ _____ _____ really, really angry, that might be 10. _____ _____ _____ .

Post-Viewing: Review
発展演習で理解を深めましょう

● Discussion

ペアやグループで意見を交換しましょう。

1. When Grace is talking with photographer David Sims about Charlie, she says, "he hates to say until Anna's seen them in case he makes a mistake." What kind of character do you think Charlie is?
2. When Charlie is talking with Tonne about Sienna's cover shot, he says, "she's kind of tough-looking in the face." Try to come up with other words to describe one's looks and compare yours with your classmates'.
3. Anna leaves a note saying "Like this best, but teeth." How do you think she feels about Sienna's teeth? Study Sienna's cover shot carefully and discuss with your classmates what is wrong with her teeth.

Grammar
動名詞と不定詞

Charlie: But I don't know if we even need <u>to reshoot</u>. But . . . um . . . it's something that's being talked about. So I just want <u>to put it in your ear</u>. I just finished <u>talking to Mario</u>. No other Nina Ricci.

動名詞句と不定詞句は動詞の補部（目的語など）になる場合があり、次のような基本的な違いがあります。

> 動名詞：実際の行動またはこれまでの経験を示す
> 不定詞：見込みのあるまたは実現可能な行動や経験を示す

この基本的な違いを意識することで、どのような動詞と結びつくかが捉えやすくなります。

❶ 動名詞句を補部にとる動詞

すでに起こったことや、今起こっていることをどうするのかという動詞が多く、消極的な動詞に多い。

admit / avoid / consider / deny / enjoy / fancy / finish / imagine / keep (on) / mind / postpone / put off / risk / stop / suggest

　　ex)　○　I **stopped** smok**ing** to get a better job.
　　　　　×　I stopped to smoke to get a better job.

❷ 不定詞句を補部にとる動詞

未来に向けて行う意欲や意図を表す動詞が多い。

afford / agree / arrange / decide / fail / hope / learn / manage / offer / plan / promise / refuse / seek / threaten

　　ex)　○　We **decided to** take a taxi home.
　　　　　×　We decided taking a taxi home.

❸ 動名詞句と不定詞句のいずれも補部にとる動詞

(1) いずれも大差なく用いられるもの

　　begin / bother / cease / continue / intend / start
　　ex)　○　It has **started** rain**ing** / **to** rain.
　　　　　○　John **intends** buy**ing** / **to** buy a house.

(2) 意味上の違いにはっきりと差があるもの

　　forget / regret / remember
　　動名詞はすでにしたことを、不定詞はこれからすることを表す。
　　ex)　I know I locked the door. I clearly **remember** lock**ing** it.
　　　　I **remembered to** lock the door, but I **forgot to** shut the windows.

(3) 不定詞だと能動、動名詞だと受動の意味になるもの

deserve / need / want

受動態の不定詞と受動の意味を持つ動名詞は置き換えが可能

ex) You **need to** lock the door.
The door **needs to** be locked.
The door **needs** [wants] lock**ing**.

● Grammar Check

( ) 内の動名詞と不定詞から適切なものを選び、○で囲んで文を完成させましょう。適切なものが複数ある場合はそれらすべてを○で囲みなさい。

1. Professor Lasnik considered (taking / to take) a train instead of a plane.

2. The majority of the reform movements sought (expanding / to expand) democratic ideals.

3. They wanted (postponing / to postpone) the vote until the September meeting.

4. If the company fails (making / to make) a profit, it will not be able to do many of the other things that a good business should do.

5. One night while I was alone in the house with my infant daughter, the baby began (crying / to cry) loudly and screaming.

6. It started (getting / to get) cold and he regretted not (wearing / to wear) his coat.

7. Everyone on our team deserves (winning / to win / to be won) the MVP.

8. You are the one that suggested (making / to make) pizza for lunch!

Unit 9
グレイスの回想

◇ 本章スクリプト→ P. 121 〜 124   DVD Ch. 9   01:11:41-01:15:59

9月号の掲載用に選ばれた写真を見てがっかりした様子のグレイスですが、過去を振り返りながらアナについて語る彼女は、やはりアナの判断力には一目置いています。ところが締め切り5日前、アナはさらにスタッフたちをざわつかせる判断を下します。

Communication Tip　　自然な会話術──疑問文のイントネーション

Warming Up
映画を視聴する前に確認しておきましょう

● **Vocabulary Check** Audio Track 26

映画の場面に出てくる語句を使って、空欄を埋めましょう。必要な場合は語形を変えてください。

> • admit　　• valid　　• request　　• urgent
> • priority　　• layout　　• filling

1. A store's _____ can have a large influence on what clothing items are sold more compared to others.
2. She _____ an extension on her essay but was denied because she had not provided the professor with enough notice.
3. _____ will be given to first-time participants in the contest. Others will have to wait.
4. My _____ fell out after eating popcorn, so I had to go to the dentist to get it repaired.
5. There is an _____ message waiting for you at the front desk, Mr. Miyake. Please come to get it as soon as possible.
6. You must provide a _____ reason for your absence from yesterday's exam in order to sit for the make-up exam.
7. Mark didn't think he'd like natto for breakfast. After he tried it, he _____ he loved it!

Viewing

場面を視聴して内容をつかみましょう

• Comprehension

次の問題の答えを選択肢から選びなさい。正解を示す場面を見て確認してみましょう。

1. **DVD** [01:12:02-01:12:25]

    Grace talks about how "Anna saw the celebrity thing coming way before everybody else jumped on that bandwagon." What does it mean "to jump on the bandwagon"?

    (A) to climb on a moving vehicle

    (B) to ignore what others are doing and do your own thing

    (C) to begin to do something that many other people are doing

    (D) none of the above

2. **DVD** [01:13:19-]

    True or false: The *Vogue* office is calm as the deadline for closing the issue approaches.

    (A) true

    (B) false

3. **DVD** [01:15:21-01:15:59]

    What parts of Sienna's body on her cover photo were discussed by Charlie and Mario?

    (A) neck, teeth, and shoulder

    (B) cheeks, teeth, and shoulder

    (C) eyebrows, teeth, and hair

    (D) neck, teeth, and hair

4. **DVD** [01:15:21-01:15:59]

    When discussing Sienna's cover photo, Charlie says, "And I'm gonna dummy it [the photo] up that way." What does it mean "to dummy something up"?

    (A) to become more stupid

    (B) to stay silent and not speak

    (C) to not change something

    (D) to make it look different

● Dictation

音声を聞いて、シナリオの空所に当てはまる英語を書き入れましょう。

① **DVD** 01:12:02-01:12:49 　　　　　　　　　　　　　　🔊 Audio Track 27

Notes

Grace: Anna saw the celebrity thing coming way before everybody else 1. _____ on that bandwagon. And, you know, whilst I hated it, I . . . I . . . I'm afraid I have to 2. _____ she was right. You know, you can't . . . you can't stay behind. You have to go charging ahead. And . . . and . . . and she did, and the magazine is very 3. _____ because of it. I mean, whilst I'd be . . . I wouldn't really care if I never saw another celebrity. 4. _____ if the magazine doesn't sell, I don't have a job, so [*laughs*]. It would be silly. [*pause*] You know, you gotta have something to put your work in, otherwise it's not 5. _____ .

whilst: [米方言] =while

② **DVD** 01:13:27-01:13:59 　　　　　　　　　　　　　　🔊 Audio Track 28

Grace: It's all change. [*chuckles*]
Woman: What?
Grace: It's all change.
Woman: What's all change?
Grace: The 6. _____ we're doing this weekend is going to be a reshoot of the color block shoot that Edward did.
Woman: What?

Grace: Anna killed color blocking. And they, they wanna
7. _____ it and then, but, of course, it's very
8. _____ , so . . .

Charlie: I got your message. We're already working on it.
Anna: Okay.
Charlie: A little while.
Anna: Okay.

Grace: I've gotta get all new clothes in five minutes.
Woman: Okay.
Grace: It's getting a little busy up here.   up here: ここまで
Woman: There's just a bunch on the 9. _____ rack.   bunch: 束
I don't know where it came from.
Man: Sarah has Marc Jacobs on her 10. _____ .   Marc Jacobs: マーク・ジェイコブス（アメリカのファッションブランド）
I'll grab that for you as well.

Post-Viewing: Review
発展演習で理解を深めましょう

● Discussion

ペアやグループで意見を交換しましょう。

1. Anna is a very forward-thinking editor, especially when she started using celebrities instead of fashion models on *Vogue*'s magazine cover. What other forward-thinking people can you think of in the arts, music, science, electronics, communications, and engineering fields? Give examples of some of their exciting ideas.

   Notes forward-thinking=forward-looking: 将来を見通した、時代を先取りする

2. As the deadline approaches for printing the magazine, many last-minute changes are being made at *Vogue*. Reflecting on your life, what times have been chaotic or busy in which you had to consider urgent matters and make priorities?

3. Charlie and Mario discuss retouching or photo manipulation of Sienna's cover photo. What are your views of magazine images being altered or changed? How do these images affect young people?

Communication Tip
自然な会話術——疑問文のイントネーション

　イントネーションとは、声の音程を上げたり、下げたり、声の高さを変えるパターンのことを言います。イントネーションは何を言うかではなく、どう言うかです。これにより、感情や態度を示すことがあります。たとえば、自分が興味を持っていること、退屈していること、ショックを受けたこと、信じられないでいることを示したりします。ここでは、イントネーションやその意味への影響に対する意識を高め、疑問文で最もよく使われるイントネーションのパターンを学びます。

　英語には異なるタイプの疑問文がありますが、今回は二つのタイプに絞って例を見ながら考えてみましょう。

(1) yes/no で答えられる疑問文　　　　　　　　🔊 Audio Track 29
　A: Are you OK?
　B: Yes, now I am. I wasn't feeling well earlier.

(2) 疑問詞を使う疑問文　　　　　　　　　　　🔊 Audio Track 30
　who, when, where, why, what, which といった wh- ではじまる語を用いた疑問文です。
　A: What time is the meeting tomorrow?
　B: It's at 9:00am.

　次に、英語で質問をするときに覚えておいたほうがよい重要な疑問文のイントネーションのルールを映画の中の台詞を例に挙げて見てみましょう。

Rule 1 yes/no で答える疑問文では、ふつう上昇調が使われる　🔊 Audio Track 31
　Grace: Have I shot that skirt ↗?
　Virginia: You shot the skirt. Yes.

Rule 2 疑問詞を使う疑問文では、ふつう下降調が使われる　🔊 Audio Track 32
　Woman: What's all change ↘?
　Grace: The shoot we're doing this weekend is going to be a reshoot of the color block shoot that Edward did.

Rule 3 驚きを表すときには、上昇調が使われる　🔊 Audio Track 33
　Grace: It's all change. [chuckles]
　Woman: What ↗?
　Grace: It's all change.

　Grace: The shoot we're doing this weekend is going to be a reshoot of the color block shoot that Edward did.
　Woman: What ↗?
　Grace: Anna killed color blocking.

Rule 4

選択肢を与える疑問文 (たとえば、"soup or salad" のように or を使うもの) では、最初の選択肢に上昇調、最後の選択肢に下降調を使う。

Woman: *Has Prada gotten this request yet ↗ or no ↘ ?*

Woman: I haven't heard back from them.

● **Task**

以下の疑問文に下降調 (↘) か上昇調 (↗) をつけなさい。音声を聞いて正解を確認してみましょう。

1. **Laurie:** And it's not gonna come in until Wednesday?　_____

2. **Grace:** Did I shoot this?　_____

3. **Mario:** What do you mean 'as of now'?　_____

4. **Grace:** What about stuff like this?　_____

5. **Mario:** Is that all I did?　_____

Unit 10
カラー・ブロッキング テイク2〜エンド・クレジット

◇ 本章スクリプト→ P. 125 〜 130　　Ch. 10-12　01:16:00-01:29:48

「カラー・ブロッキング特集」の再撮影、写真のチェックや修正を経て、ついに『VOGUE』9月号が刊行されます。締め切り間際まで紆余曲折ありましたが、一体どんな仕上がりになるのでしょう。そして、最終的に誌面に並んだ写真は……？　最後にアナが語ります。

| **Culture** | ジャズ・エイジ（Jazz Age） |

Warming Up
映画を視聴する前に確認しておきましょう

● Vocabulary Check
 Audio Track 36

映画の場面に出てくる語句を使って、空欄を埋めましょう。必要な場合は語形を変えてください。

> - dense　　● accessible　● props　　● singular
> - pretentious　● authority　● decisiveness

1. We used a strong color contrast to make it more _____ to people with low vision.

2. It was very unwise of you to overstep your _____ .

3. She showed more _____ than we usually expected from a leader.

4. Full of stylistic experiments, James Joyce's *Ulysses* is considered to be a _____ text.

5. They made their living producing _____ for film and television.

6. The editor is known for her dislike of wine experts' _____ language that, in her view, no one understands.

7. We appreciate the _____ beauty of these cultural artifacts in this museum.

Viewing

場面を視聴して内容をつかみましょう

● Comprehension

次の問題の答えを選択肢から選びなさい。正解を示す場面を見て確認してみましょう。

1. **DVD** | 01:16:41-01:18:37 |

   What does Anna mean by "a breath of fresh air"?

   (A) a section that makes you relaxed
   (B) an image that embodies an original idea
   (C) a break for refreshments
   (D) a day off from work

2. **DVD** | 01:20:56-01:21:04 |

   What does Charlie mean by "fix[ing]" Sienna's neck?

   (A) doing a surgical operation on her neck
   (B) altering the image of her neck
   (C) changing her necklace
   (D) putting more make-up on her neck

3. **DVD** | 01:21:04-01:21:21 |

   What can be inferred from Anna's remark "Looks like it's for blind people"?

   (A) She admired the typesetter who cares for people with visual impairments.
   (B) She was dazzled by the flashy style of the cover.
   (C) She is always politically correct.
   (D) She found the gaudy type distasteful.

4. **DVD** | 01:22:31-01:23:17 |

   How is Grace probably feeling when she says, "Wasn't Sienna originally the lead?"

   (A) unpleasantly surprised
   (B) pleasantly surprised
   (C) infuriated
   (D) amused

● **Dictation**

音声を聞いて、シナリオの空所に当てはまる英語を書き入れましょう。

① 01:19:09-01:19:57   Audio Track 37

Notes

retouch: 画像を修正する
I bet = I'm sure

Grace: Did she like them?
Bob: "A bit of retouching," she said.
Grace: Oh, I bet. [*laughs*] Of course.
Bob: She told me I needed to go to the gym.
Grace: Uh . . . 1. _____ _____ which picture? The jumping one?
Bob: Yeah. She's right.
Grace: No, but, it . . . I . . . you know, 2. _____ , I think it's better that you're not, like, skinny, skinny. I really . . . To me, it's much more, makes 3. _____ _____ than . . . that you're real people and not . . . models. Everybody isn't 4. _____ in this world. I mean, it's enough that the models are 4. _____ . You don't need to go to the gym. [*laughs*]

② 01:23:36-01:24:10   Audio Track 38

Anna: [*To the interviewer*] I don't believe for one minute that I have 5. ____ _____ ____ what's gonna happen or 5. ____ _____ ____ real change the way Grace does. I mean, Grace's a 6. _____ , and there is

no one that can visualize a picture or understand the . . . the 7. _____ of fashion or . . . produce a great shoot. I mean, she's just 8. _____ .
[*To her assistant*] Okay. [*To the interviewer*] She and I don't always agree, but I think that over the years we've learned how to 9. _____ _____ each other's different 10. _____ _____ _____ .

Post-Viewing: Review
発展演習で理解を深めましょう

● Discussion

ペアやグループで意見を交換しましょう。

1. Anna and Grace have very different opinions about the weight and the body shape of people in fashion magazines. Who do you agree with? Why?
2. How would you describe Anna's relationship with Grace?
3. Anna says, "Fashion is not about looking back. It's always about looking forward." She always thinks ahead, but recycled old images in this particular issue. That points to a contradiction in fashion: "Fashion is obsessed with the new, yet it continually harks to the past" (Rebecca Arnold). What do you think of this contradiction?

   Notes hark to: 〜に言及する、〜を回顧する

Culture
ジャズ・エイジ（Jazz Age）

　　Anna: We . . . uh . . . had the idea to do a sort of Jazz Age shoot.

　『VOGUE』2007年9月号のコンセプトについて、アナは上記のように言っています。Jazz Age とは、アメリカの繁栄や若者の狂騒、性風俗の変化に特徴付けられた1920年代を指します。
　この表現は、アメリカの小説家F・スコット・フィッツジェラルドの *The Tales of Jazz Age* (1922) に由来します。彼は Jazz Age を代表する作家で、その言葉はこの時代の雰囲気を伝えてくれます。たとえば、この短編集に収録された "The Diamond as Big as the Ritz" の末尾には、こんな文章があります。

① 日本語に訳してみましょう。
　At any rate, let us love for a while, for a year or so, you and me. That's a form of divine drunkenness that we can all try. There are only diamonds in the whole world, diamonds and perhaps the shabby gift of disillusion. Well, I have that last and I will make the usual nothing of it.
　Notes　shabby: 粗末な、つまらぬ　disillusion: 幻滅

　フィッツジェラルドの代表作『偉大なるギャツビー』(1925) は、アメリカン・ドリームとその末路を描いた傑作で、何度か映画化されています。特に有名なのはロバート・レッドフォード主演の作品 (1974) とレオナルド・ディカプリオ主演の作品 (2013) でしょう。一代にして財をなしたジェイ・ギャツビーの生き様が、田舎出身の青年ニック・キャラウェイの視点から語られます。
　この作品には、華やかなだけではないこの時代の暗い側面も描かれています。ギャツビーの敵役となるトム・ブキャナンは、ロスロップ・ストッダードの *The Rising Tide of Color Against White World-Supremacy* (1920) という著述を絶賛し、そのうえでこのように言います。

② 日本語に訳してみましょう。
It's up to us, who are the dominant race, to watch out or these other races will have control of things.

_____

_____

_____

　これは優生学（eugenics）と呼ばれる考え方で、当時アメリカで流行していました。優秀な遺伝子を残そうとする考え方なのですが、これは往々にして白人優位主義や人種差別、障がい者たちへの差別につながりました。
　一見すると明るくて夢のある時代ですが、そのような暗い側面もあったのです。

● Research Activities

Jazz Age について調べてみましょう。当時のファッションやサブカルチャーは、現代の文化にどのように残っていたり、パロディされていたりするでしょうか。

Transcript

Unit 1
New York City 2007

DVD Ch. 1 00:00:08-00:08:26

(Speaking to camera - Anna Wintour) 00:00:08-

Anna: I … I think what … I … I often see is that people are 1._____ of fashion and that … because it scares them or makes them feel 2._____, they put it down.
5 On the 3._____, people that say demeaning things about … uh … our world, I think that's usually because they feel, in some ways, 4._____ or, you know, not part of the cool group or … So, as a result, they … they just 5._____ it. Just because you like to put on a
10 beautiful Carolina Herrera dress or a—I don't know— pair of J Brand blue jeans, that you know, instead of something basic from K-Mart, it doesn't mean that you're a … a dumb person.
There is something about fashion that can make people
15 very 6._____.

demeaning: 恥ずべき

Carolina Herrera: キャロリーナ・ヘレラ（ベネズエラ出身で、母娘同名という2名のデザイナーによるブランド）
J Brand: アメリカ発のデニム・ブランド
K-Mart: アメリカのディスカウントストア・チェーン
dumb: 物言わぬ ※「役に立たない」を含意する

(In a Cab. Talking on her phone - Anna Wintour) 00:01:14-

Anna: Uh. Sophie, hi. This email here from Tom Ford. Can you send it on to Jay? Okay, thanks.

Tom Ford: アメリカのデザイナーで映画監督

AT ANNA'S OFFICE - *VOGUE* 00:01:30-

20 **Woman:** Anna Wintour's office.

Woman=Assistant of Anna

Edward: Kate, there's a bit of a crisis.
Woman: Kate … full of … top of things.
Edward: Anna saw the pictures, and she doesn't want Chanel or

Transcript

		Hilary. Okay, bye. So, I think we're done with Hilary and Chanel.
	Grace:	I wonder if Anna would like this one.
	Candy:	Well, it's black.
5	**Grace**:	That's true. I'd get fired for that.
	Candy:	These are the approved ones that Mark and I showed Anna. But also Anna did not like the landing page, and we have redesigned it, and that's what we're showing Anna tomorrow.
10	**Woman**:	Okay.

(Speaking to camera – Candy Pratts) 00:02:32-

	Candy:	It is always going to be Anna's point of view. *Vogue* is Anna's magazine. That's who signs it off. We know that. You belong to it. You belong to this church.
15	**Interviewer**:	And is it fair to say that Anna is the high priestess of all of us?
	Candy:	I would say "Pope."
	Tom:	L'Oréal's meeting with Anna to talk about having the designers design an infallible dress.
20	**Woman**:	[*Chuckles*]
	Woman:	That's perfect.

(Speaking to camera – Tom Florio) 00:03:03-

	Tom:	She sees her role as the director and producer of this fashion world.
25	**Interviewer**:	Can you think of an aspect of the fashion industry that she isn't somehow involved in?
	Tom:	No.

Hilary: アメリカの女優ヒラリー・ダフはデザイナーとしてDKNYジーンズのセカンドラインを発表。

landing page:（読者が）最初に開くページ

signs ... off: …を終わらせる

high priestess: 女教皇　※priestの女性形

L'Oréal: ロレアル パリ（世界最大のビューティ・ブランド）

FASHION WEEK, NEW YORK CITY 00:03:17-

André: We have to see clothes. First of all, it's been a very bleak week so far. It's been bleak street over here in America.

5 **Vera**: You know.

André: You know what? It's a famine of beauty.

Vera: Right. We're gonna have some beauty.

André: It's a famine of beauty. It's a famine of beauty, honey. My eyes are starving for beauty.

10 **Asian Man**: More wild.

Woman: You don't have to go too fast, but good energy, good confidence.

Woman: Is Anna here already?

Vera: Julie, uh … they're wondering is Anna here yet?

15 **André**: Vera, she's there.

Woman: We're ready to start. Here we go. We're gonna go.

SHOW STARTS 00:03:51-

MC: I'm with the internationally renowned editor-in-chief of American *Vogue*, Anna Wintour.

20 **Man1**: Anna Wintour, the editor-in-chief of *Vogue* magazine, a bible for the fashion world …

Man2: The single most important figure in the $300 billion global fashion industry.

Woman: She is watched more closely than the movie stars or
25 the runway.

Journalist 1: Anna. Many people said that you are an "ice woman."

Anna: Well, this week, it was pretty cold. That's all I can say. [*laughs*]

bleak: わびしい、陰気な

starve for: …を渇望する、…に飢える

Transcript

FASHION WEEK - PARIS 00:04:52-

(A couple of people call her "Anna")

Karl Lagerfeld: Ah, voilà. Anna, look. This one we call "Anna" anyway.

5 **Someone**: Voilà.

Woman: Is it?

Bee: [*Chuckles*]

Anna: It's gorgeous.

Camera Man: Anna.

10 **Man**: Is there a way to wear fur this winter?

Anna: There is always a way to wear fur. Personally, I have it on my back. [*Chuckles*]

Interviewer: What is your role at this défilé? Will you explain?

André: What is my role at the défilé? To help Anna Wintour
15   decide what goes in the magazine and to help the editors of *Vogue* to have a dialogue about fashion.

Journalist 2: Anna a le plus grand pouvoir sur les femmes aux États-Unis.

André: Oui. Absolument.

20 *(Title shows "The September Issue")*

AT YVES SAINT LAURENT 00:06:30-

Anna: Hi, Stefano.

Stefano: Hi, Anna, how are you?

Anna: I'm well.

25 **Stefano**: Good to see you.

Anna: How are things?

Stefano: Uh, well. Shall I tell you the truth? [*chuckles*]

Anna: Yeah.

Voilà: [仏]（注意を引いて）見て、ほら

défilé: [仏]ファッションショー

Anna a le plus grand pouvoir sur les femmes aux États-Unis.: [仏] = Anna has the greatest influence over women in the United States.

Oui. Absolument: [仏] = Yeah. Absolutely.

	Stefano:	I'm a bit stressed this season.
	Anna:	You're stressed?
	Stefano:	A bit. A bit.
	Anna:	Oh.
5	**Stefano**:	But I hope it's going to be okay.
	Hamish:	Hello.
	Woman:	Hello.
	Hamish:	Good to see you.
	Woman:	Good to see you too.
10	**Anna**:	Stefano, can we start?
	Stefano:	Yes. OK. [*chuckles*] Anna. Is this? … I'll show them three by three. So, this is look number one. OK, you just walk around easily. Voilà. So, this season, basically what I decided to work on is to go back to the
15		7._____ of the cut. Everything is hand-stitched, all around.
	Hamish:	Wow.
	Anna:	I don't see any real evening on that 8._____. Are you not doing it?
20	**Stefano**:	No. I am …
	Anna:	But?
	Stefano:	But they're all …
	Anna:	In pieces? Do we have sketches?
25	**Stefano**:	Yes … I have one cocktail dress. But this is the workmanship, which is this one. No. Did you see that, no?
	Anna:	No, that's pretty. So, you're not really feeling for color, Stefano.
30	**Stefano**:	No. No. No. You know, it's … it's … it's my 9._____. I mean, in winter, I never feel so much for color. It's more it's more a summer thing for me, frankly speaking, but … it's a bit 10._____. New … blacks. I don't know. There's blue navy. There is … there is an emerald

three by three : 3 点ずつ ※one by one: 一つずつ

hand-stitched: 手縫いする

evening=evening dress

cocktail dress: パーティ等で着る婦人服。イブニングドレスよりもカジュアルなものを指す。
workmanship: (職人の)技量

Transcript

		green. [*chuckles*] You know.
	Anna:	Very colorful.
	Stefano:	This is colorful.
	Virginia:	Okay, I'm gonna need you when I'm convincing Anna
5		that that's not black. We have green, navy …

Transcript

Unit 2
Vogue Retailers Breakfast

Ch. 2 00:08:27-00:17:14

Anna:	Hi.	
Burton:	Good morning. Good morning. How are you?	
Anna:	Good. I'm fine.	
Woman:	You look beautiful.	
5 **Burton**:	Are you wearing Chanel?	
Anna:	Yes. Trying to look like your customer.	
Burton:	[*chuckles*] You are our customer. So we'll follow you.	
Anna:	Yes.	
Burton:	Well, thank you for continuing these breakfasts. I speak	
10	for the group, they're very helpful, and … and continue	
	to allow us to get to know each other better and better,	
	and … uh … we thank you for your time.	
Anna:	So, I'm going to ask Sally to start talking about our main	
	points.	
15 **Sally**:	The … the key item for us, it seems to be, is the jacket.	
Burton:	Absolutely right.	
Anna:	We're going to be putting a huge, huge push onto a	
	wardrobe of jackets for … for the fall issues.	

a wardrobe of: 〜の衣装（全部）

(Speaking to camera – Tom Florio) 00:09:07-

20 **Tom**: Nobody was wearing fur until Anna put it back on the cover of *Vogue* back in the early nineties, and she ignited the entire industry. If we get behind something, it sells.

Virginia: For once, Prada was in great debate this season. Anna

Prada: プラダ（イタリアを代表するファッションブランド）

		had a lot of concerns over the fabric and s … spoke with Mrs. Prada on your behalf many times.
	Anna:	We felt that the pieces were just so heavy that you couldn't wear it. So, Virginia, what was it that they're going to reinterpret? 'Cause we really pushed.
	Virginia:	They did tell me that they are doing … um … a version of a fabric that's silk and mohair as opposed to the heavy wool and mohair. It's a degrade fabric.
	Karen:	Fantastic.
10	**Anna**:	Thank you. Good.
	Karen:	You've made our week, our three weeks.
	Burton:	Well. Let me touch on something that may be out of your purview, but, maybe you can also help us. Uh … deliveries of merchandise.
15	*(Everybody laughs)*	
	Anna:	What do you want me to do about that? Rent a truck?
	Burton:	Tell you what I'd like you to do. You … you are so influential with the designers.
	Anna:	[*chuckles*] Not that.
20	**Burton**:	They have to recognize that the worldwide demand for their product is expanding at a rate that even they don't understand, and they're not keeping up with the production so that the … the demand is outstripping supply. We're waiting longer and longer and longer for deliveries. They're coming at the back end of the delivery schedule instead of the front end. And, you know, fashion is fun, and we all love it, and that's what drives it, but …
	Anna:	You want it now.
30	**Burton**:	… without the goods … Without the goods … and the ads in your magazines are fabulous, and I know you'll look like a telephone book this year, but …
	(Everybody laughs)	

Mrs. Prada: ミウッチャ・プラダ(Miuccia Prada)のこと。プラダの創業者マリオ・プラダの孫。

mohair: モヘア(アンゴラヤギの毛)
degrade: 質を落とした

	Burton:	Uh … We gotta … You've gotta help us with this, so you have a couple of choices.
	Anna:	I think …
	Burton:	You can start sewing yourselves.
5	**Anna**:	Mm … hmm. No, I think you said something very interesting about, which is editing. And I think some of the designers do have a problem with that, and we are working on that, and we will certainly … We're right there with you. Less is more.

Less is more.: 少なければ少ないほど効果は増す。

10 **VOGUE OFFICES – TIMES SQUARE, NEW YORK** 00:11:04-

	Grace:	I mean, I can't shoot everything for the rest of my life with Steven Meiseil in Alder Mansion, which is an ugly fucking house.
	Edward:	I was discussing my September shoot with Steven
15		Klein.
	Anna:	Mm … hmm.
	Edward:	I think he really likes this location.
	Anna:	It's sort of gloomy, Edward. Where's the glamour?
	Edward:	Um …
20	**Anna**:	It's *Vogue*, okay? Please, let's …
	Edward:	Lift it.
	Anna:	Lift it.

Steven Meiseil: スティーヴン・マイゼル（NY出身の写真家）

Steven Klein: スティーヴン・クライン（米ロードアイランド出身の写真家）

gloomy: 暗い、陰気な
glamour:（服の着こなしなど全体的な）魅力

Lift it.: 品位を高めて

(Speaking to camera – Tom Florio) 00:11:36-

	Tom:	I don't find her to be hidden. I just don't find her to be
25		accessible to people she doesn't need to be accessible to.
	Anna:	This, I don't think we need. This is … We'll just wait for whatever it is they're making …
	Virginia:	Okay.
	Anna:	And that's it. This, I don't think we should do.
30	**Virginia**:	Okay.
	Anna:	This, I don't think we should do. This.

Transcript

Tom:	She's busy, [*chuckles*] you know. And she's not warm and friendly. She's doing her business.	

Anna:	These are all horrible.	
Charlie:	Yes.	
5	**Anna**:	I thought this was pretty weak.	**pretty:**[皮肉的に]かなり、ひどく
Charlie:	It is.	
Anna:	That stuff needed a lot of work.	
Charlie:	Okay.	
Anna:	All right?	
10 | **Charlie**: | Yes. | |

Tom:	We leave warm to me. I'll have to be warm enough for the two of us.

VOGUE ADVERTISING SALES TEAM
– SEPTEMBER KICK-OFF MEETING 00:12:12-

15 **Tom**: When we put out the September issue of *Vogue*, the first thing the reporters usually ask us is how much does it 1._____ and how many pages? 2._____ _____ _____ American 3._____, almost thirteen million people, will get that issue. A few
20 years ago when we put out a record issue of September, it was the largest monthly magazine ever published. Guys, we're looking to break that record. We have to break 4._____ _____. I want you to go into it like it's *Vogue* the brand and market it like it's
25 never been 5._____ in its entire 114 years.

Anna: All right, so, September. Sienna, I think we're in excellent shape, right?

	Tonne:	It's all feathers.	
	Virginia:	I think this is really cute.	
	Tonne:	I do, too.	
	Virginia:	Do you?	
5	**Tonne**:	Big Bird.	**Big Bird:** 教育テレビ番組『セサミストリート』に登場する大きな黄色い鳥

(Speaking to camera – Tonne Goodman) `00:13:00-`

Tonne: The team sees the collections and then comes back and has fashion meetings, and in the meetings, you dissect the collections and decide what trends to feature.

10	**Anne**:	André, I hear you didn't like Calvin.	**Calvin=Calvin Klein:** カルバン·クライン(アメリカのファッションデザイナー)
	André:	I thought it was clinical.	
	Grace:	[*Chuckles*]	
	André:	I said … impolite.	**impolite:** 無礼な

(Speaking to camera – Candy Pratts) `00:13:15-`

15 **Candy**: September is the January in fashion, you know? This is when I change. This is when I say, you know, I'm gonna try to get back on those high heels … 'cause, okay, that's the look.

look: (流行の)型、デザイン

Sally: Yeah, the jacket is the new coat.

20 **Candy**: The look is sexy. The look is granny. You need to know.

granny: 老婦人好みのスタイルの

	Tonne:	This is heaven. That's gorgeous.	
	Grace:	That should be a fashion story.	
	Anna:	Well, that's … but that's the problem, Grace. It's an accessory story, and that's what I need.	
25	**Grace**:	Well, it's a story crying to be done.	**cry to do:** 〜する必要がある
	Anna:	Grace, I hear you, but it's just not what I need in the September issue.	

Transcript

(Speaking to camera – Sally) `00:13:46-`

Sally: You have to really find some stories there. And you have to find stories that haven't been played out anywhere else, and they have to be on a certain scale.

---

5 **Anna**: Having talked to Grace a little bit about this, I think she very much wants to do texture.

Virginia: [*chuckles*]
Anna: What has that got to do with texture?
Virginia: [*chuckles*]
10 **Grace**: Well, look.
Anna: No.

Woman: I think you should bring it anyway.
Grace: It's breaking my heart. Usually in the September issue, there's one big disaster. There's always one shoot that's
15 a big problem in the issue, because it's a big issue and there's a lot of things going on.

FIVE MONTHS UNTIL ISSUE CLOSES `00:14:20-`

Anna: Let's put that one to the side for now. And that one, too. Let me see what else there is.
20 **Virginia**: Jonathan Saunders is someone we wanted to— … I mean …
Edward: We're trying to get him in.
Anna: It's cute, but it's a different thing.
Virginia: What difference is that?
25 **Edward**: Hmm.
Anna: They're not color blocking.
Edward: Hmm. I wanna kill myself.
Grace: You wanna kill yourself?

> Jonathan Saunders: ジョナサン・サンダース(イギリス人のファッションデザイナー)

Edward: Yeah.

Grace: Why?

Edward: I don't know what I'm doing anymore.

Grace: What's happened?

5 **Edward**: This got thrown out.

Grace: If it's with this.

Edward: This is what we did.

Grace: It's fine.

Edward: It wasn't the look. She said no.

10 **Grace**: Color blocking's all the different colors. It's, see, you know, this with this and this with this, and …

Edward: I'm gonna take this anyway.

Grace: Is that the best one? That's not the best one. You've gotta be tougher. Edward.

15 **Edward**: Tell me, what do you do?

Grace: You gotta be tough.

Edward: What'd you do?

Grace: You gotta just … just demand. You have to demand. Because o … otherwise you'll be blamed. Don't be too

20 nice. Even to me. [*chuckles*] No, honestly, because you'll lose. You have to learn the way to 6._____ your path through to make yourself 7._____ and make yourself necessary and find a way that works for you, for *Vogue* because a lot of people have come and a lot

25 of people have gone. They just couldn't take the 8._____. You know, you have to be 9._____ tough to 10._____ that.

Anna: So it's all pinks.

Elissa: Mm … hmm. And Virginia …

30 **Anna**: Do we really feel that this is the most important message to put in the September issue?

Virginia: I loved it.

Transcript

	Elissa:	It's important.	
	Virginia:	I thought it was pretty.	
	Anna:	It looks very springy.	**springy:** 軽快な
	Elissa:	Well, there's fur.	
5	**Anna**:	Maybe you wanna develop it a little bit more, and I'd also like to see what you're thinking about with the clothes, so I can get more of a handle on it.	
	Elissa:	I was thinking maybe it's kind of body conscious for clothes.	
	Virginia:	Mm … hmm …	
10	**Elissa**:	And then at one point, I thought maybe she could be sort of bionic. It looks good on the rack.	**sort of:**(形容詞などを修飾して）むしろ、多少、大体
	Anna:	I feel it's quite one-dimensional. But also, the girls always look the same, Elissa.	**one-dimensional:** 深みのない、単調な
	Elissa:	What do you mean?	
15	**Anna**:	If you look at your pictures, the way they're dressed, it's always the same. And somehow, the picture's always the same. It's usually the same kind of minimal approach.	**minimal:** 最小限の、ミニマルアートの
	Elissa:	Okay. All right.	
20	**Anna**:	I mean, it's … it's what you are, I know. And the girl always tends to have straight hair [*Chuckles*].	
	Elissa:	Yeah.	
	Anna:	If you look at it yourself, just like, it's always the same. So it would be great if we could break out. Thanks. So you know that company, Mango, in Spain?	**break out:**(旧習などから）脱け出す **Mango:** スペイン発のファストファッション・ブランド
25	**Virginia**:	Yes.	
	Anna:	They're looking for someone to help them consult.	
	Virginia:	Mm … hmm.	
	Anna:	Maybe Thakoon, you think?	
	Virginia:	I think he's one of the most talented people out there.	
30	**Anna**:	He's coming in to see me, I think, this week, so I could talk to him.	
	Virginia:	Okay.	
	Anna:	Okay.	

Transcript

Unit 3
Anna's History

 Ch. 3 00:17:15-00:27:26

	Anna:	So, Yuri, can we stop at Starbucks, please? My father was a newspaper editor. He edited a newspaper in London called *The Evening Standard*.
	(TV Audio):	Former Fleet Street editor, Charles Wintour, will be
5		assessing the long-term effects.
	Anna:	He came from quite a Victorian upbringing. I'm not sure his mother ever spoke to him. He was also very private and very, in some ways, inscrutable.
	(TV Audio):	The NPA have about as much collective spine as a
10		tepid jellyfish.
	Anna:	Growing up in London in the sixties, I mean, you'd have to be walking around with Irving Penn's sack over your head not to know that something extraordinary was happening in fashion. The look of the girls then and
15		everything that was going on, the pill and emancipation of women and the end of the class system and just sort of seeing that revolution go on, made me love it from an early age.
		I think my father really decided for me that I should
20		work in fashion. I can't remember what form it was I had to fill out. Maybe it was an admissions thing, and at the bottom, it said 'Career objectives,' you know, and I looked at it and said, 'What shall I do? How shall I fill this out?' And he said, 'Well, you write that you want to
25		be editor of *Vogue*, of course.' So, that was it. It was decided.

Notes

The Evening Standard: ロンドンで発行している無料のタブロイド日刊新聞
Fleet Street: ロンドンの新聞界
Victorian: ヴィクトリア女王時代(19世紀)の、旧式の
upbringing: (幼少期の)しつけ、教育
inscrutable: 計り知れない、謎めいた
NPA=Newspaper Publishers' Association: (英国の)新聞発行者協会
spine: 背骨、気骨
tepid: なまぬるい
jellyfish: クラゲ
Irving Penn: アーヴィング・ペン(アメリカの写真家。長年『VOGUE』のファッション写真の撮影を手がけた)

class system: 階級制度

career objectives: 職業目的

Transcript

	Anna:	We have known about this piece for a long time. So I don't ... don't wanna hear it, okay? I mean, she should just get on the phone.
5		This is not clear. Somebody needs to check these. She looks pregnant. We need to ...
	Man:	... Fix her.
	Anna:	Yeah.

Thakoon Speaking in a Cab 00:19:29-

	Thakoon:	The first time that you're asked to go see Anna and
10		show her your collection, it's like ... insane.
	Woman:	Intimidating. Right.
	Thakoon:	And I remember there was me and Meredith in Anna's office. It was the first time I met her. I was, like, oh, my God, it's Anna. It's, like, Madonna is Anna, do you
15		know?
	Woman:	Yeah.
	Thakoon:	And I was just—She's like, 'Okay, go on.' So I'm, like, talking about the inspiration. Like, I'm moving my hands, and I'm, like, showing her, you know, the pieces. And I
20		can see my hand, like, shaking. It was, like, shaking. Because she just sat there the whole time, like, 'Mm-hmm, mm-hmm.' So then we, we get out of there, and Meredith's like, 'Oh, my God, you were so well-spoken, but that hand kept shaking.'
25	**Woman**:	Oh.

Anna's Office 00:20:13-

	Woman:	Anna Wintour's office.
	Anna:	Hi, Thakoon. How are you?
	Thakoon:	Hi, how are you? I have eight sketches. I don't know
30		how you want me to lay them out for you.
	Jill:	Right here.

Meredith= Meredith Melling-Burke: メレディス・メリング・バーク(『VOGUE』のシニア・マーケット・エディター)

Thakoon: Okay.
Anna: You know Thakoon, right?
Woman: Yes, nice to see you.
Thakoon: Yes.
Anna: So these are his sketches for the Gap project, the shirts.
Jill: Mm … hmm. And it's three that would—
Anna: We're meant to narrow it down to three?
Woman: Mm … hmm.
Anna: I think we ought to do one with a little sleeve.
Woman: I love the little sleeve.
Anna: And then maybe one that's a dress.

Sally: It's very hard to be a 1._____ in this country. So we created a fashion fund to draw attention to new 2._____, to fund it, and to … and to get mentoring for it. The winners get to design something for a mega-brand.
Anna: You like this one?
Tonne: I wouldn't discount that. It's got a simplicity that the Gap 3._____ is going to immediately acknowledge.

Sally: Thakoon was one of the winners of the award. He has all the 4._____ to have a serious high-end designer line.

Anna: I'm happy with those three. Perfect. All right. Well, thank you.
Thakoon: Thank you.

Sally: You never know, though. I mean, remember Isaac Mizrahi went out of business. The fashion 5._____ isn't fair. They do everything right, and they still crash.

Gap: 米最大の衣料品製造小売業チェーン

be meant to …: …しなければならない
narrow down to …: …に制限する、しぼる

Isaac Mizrahi: アイザック・ミズラヒ（アメリカの実力派ファッションデザイナー）

Transcript

TEXTURE SHOOT 00:21:31-

Grace: Those colors are good. I'm one of the last remaining fashion editors who dress the girls myself. I'm told the very modern thing is to don't touch the girl. Is that right? Yeah. Who does it?

Model: No.

Grace: An assistant?

Model: Yeah.

Grace: I don't know. I'm a bit old-fashioned.

Model: [*Chuckles*]

Grace: I love this. See? I love this.

Camera man: Good, Coco. Watch the light, guys. Come on.

Grace: She just looks like she's got a plastic bag on. But it looks good. Garbage bag or something.

Women: Good night.

Camera man: Good night, everyone.

(Speaking to camera – Grace) 00:22:34-

Grace: Well, I started reading *Vogue* when I was a teenager, and I grew up in north Wales. And it was kind … uh … of difficult to get. So I used to order it and rush once a month to get my copy, which was probably three months out of date. I loved the whole sort of chic thing that was so entirely out of context compared to the lifestyle I led. You know, I went to school. I went to a convent. I never went anywhere for my holidays, and so I just looked at *Vogue*.

At the same time, there was a *Vogue* model competition, and somebody sent my … pic … very bad pictures in. And I actually won the young section. 'Cause I was quite young at that time. And so I started modeling for *Vogue*.

Wales: ウェールズ（イギリス、グレートブリテン島の南西部を占める地域）

chic: 粋な、あかぬけた

convent: 修道院

Somehow everything I did, I kind of fell into. I just knew that I probably had to get out of that place. So I went up to London, and I became a full-time model.

5 These are the pictures of me by various photographers. This is one of my very first model pictures. Um … It's probably um … '59 by Lord Snowdon. I stopped modeling because I had a car crash. Um … My head went into the driving mirror, or my eye went into the driving mirror. So I had a lot of plastic surgery. And …
10 um … then two years later, I sort of went back to work.

This is from a shoot that I did with Bailey, Helmut. This is Manolo Blahnik, and this is Anjelica Huston when she was modeling. I was offered a job at British *Vogue*. I was a junior editor, and … um … kind of slowly worked
15 my way up.

VOGUE OFFICE 00:24:50-

Grace: Hello.
Virginia: Ms. Coddington.
Grace: Oh, my God.
20 **Virginia**: How was your shoot?
Grace: It was great. It was great.

Sally: This is really good, isn't it?
Woman: Good, aren't they?
Man: Who styled that?
25 **Woman**: Grace, right?
Man: Grace and Craig.
Sally: It's real nice.
Man: It's beautiful.

Lord Snowdon: 初代スノードン伯爵アンソニー・アームストロング=ジョーンズ（イギリスの写真家）

plastic surgery: 整形外科

Bailey: クリストファー・ベイリー（イギリス出身のファッションデザイナー）
Helmut: ヘルムート・ラング（ウィーン生まれのデザイナー）
Manolo Blahnik: マノロ・ブラニク（イギリス発の高級靴ブランド）
Anjelica Huston: アンジェリカ・ヒューストン（アメリカの女優。映画監督のジョン・ヒューストンを父に、俳優のウォルター・ヒューストンを祖父に持つ）

Transcript

(Speaking to camera – Sally) `00:25:31-`

Sally: Grace is without question the greatest living 6._____. There's no one better than Grace. There's no one who can make any 7._____ take more beautiful, more interesting, more romantic, more just 8._____ realized pictures than Grace. There … there abso … there's no one better. Period. She comes from the idea that fashion is this world of play and 9._____-_____. It's … it's … as if someone's gone to the 10._____-_____ box and found the most kind of wonderful, personal things, and put them together, but it's beautiful.

Period.: [米口語] (以上)終わり。

VOGUE OFFICE `00:26:03-`

Danko: Hi, Anna.

Anna: Hi. I'm not crazy about this one, are you?

Danko: I like it.

Anna: Do we need this? It's just not saying texture to me. All the others, I—Do you understand what I'm saying?

Danko: Yeah.

Anna: I'm just really, really concerned about how much black we're getting. So, if we were to take another one out?

Danko: Maybe that?

Anna: Let me see it.

Danko: Okay.

Anna: Let me just see it.

Danko: Okay.

Anna: Okay. Whose is that?

Danko: I think it's Rodarte.

Grace: What have they snipped off here? Which one went? That's the guess. Oh, yes, of course, the other black one. Those poor goddamn Rodartes.

crazy about: …が大好きだ、…に夢中だ

Rodarte: ロダルテ（アメリカのファッションブランド）

goddamn: ひどい

Danko: I know. They're … They're out.

Grace: Rubber's not a texture?

Danko: No, not for Anna.

Grace: And leather's definitely—

5 **Danko**: We ordered it. We order all the prints, so …

Grace: Oh, yeah, I've heard that story.

Danko: Yeah.

Grace: But it's such a great picture, that.

Danko: Yeah. Anna actually liked it as a picture. She thought it
10 wasn't texture.

Grace: It is texture.

rubber: ゴム製の

Transcript

Unit 4
Thakoon & Oscar

Ch. 4 00:27:27–00:36:15

Thakoon:	Let's add the waist seam now then. Do we need pockets?	
Anna:	So … this one is … is it not around?	
Oscar:	Yes, it is. I think.	
5 **Anna**:	Fabulous color. I personally would not put this one in the show, but the other things you've shown us are more exciting.	
Oscar:	All of this, actually, is still under consideration.	
Virginia:	You need to have a hundred there, no?	
10 **Oscar**:	Listen, we have a hundred and fifty pieces, and we have to edit them down to sixty-five.	
Anna:	Grace is very good at that. Go on, Grace.	
Grace:	[laughs]	
Anna:	Slash and burn.	
15 **Grace**:	No, Anna's, but I don't think you could take Anna's … slashing. [laughs]	
Oscar:	So … That's the man from … from Mango.	
Anna:	Oh.	
Oscar:	Who do you think would be good?	
20 **Anna**:	Thakoon.	
Oscar:	And apparently they pay extremely well. And perhaps they want to … I'm going to propose you and me. [chuckles] Who is … who is this … this, Anna?	
Anna:	Thakoon.	
25 **Oscar**:	Mm … hmm.	
Anna:	He's really good.	

Notes
seam:(布・皮などの)縫い目

edit … down to ~:
…を~まで編集する

Thakoon: See, now it's beautiful. Now it's really pretty, it is.

André: This is good. This is good.

Elissa: So, for the brooch.
Virginia: Lanvin.
5 **Elissa**: We have this. It's from Balenciaga. I think it's cool.
Anna: It's like a neck brace.
Elissa: At first we thought maybe it was a scarf.
Anna: It's a neck brace.
Elissa: Yeah.

10 *(Speaking to camera – Grace)* 00:29:49-

Grace: I moved on. I'm onto twenties now. Twenties is something that … Well, really the inspiration was John Galliano's show. He was 1._____ by the photographer Brassaï, who was a photographer from
15 the twenties. Shoes, I'm very 2._____ _____. It just has to be something that 3._____ evokes the twenties. What has she got? Well. You have to have that fashion story, you know, spots are in or stripes or full skirts or straight skirts or whatever it is. But I've tried
20 to make that 4._____. We build a fantasy around the girl and what she's doing, what she's thinking, who she is.

VOGUE OFFICE 00:30:34-

Woman: But there, you know.
25 **Grace**: Yeah, that. But, of course, what's so genius about that is that, you know, she has big, fat legs and things. I love that.
Woman: This is … It's a reference picture as well.

Lanvin: ランバン(フランス発のファッションブランド)
Balenciaga: バレンシアガ(バスク系スペイン人デザイナーによるパリのファッションブランド)

John Galliano: ジョン・ガリアーノ(イギリスのファッションデザイナー)
Brassaï: ブラッサイ(ハンガリー出身の写真家。パリで活躍した)

Transcript

	Grace:	They're so beautiful.
	Anna:	Okay. Are they coming for the run-through, please?
	Woman:	That was just Anna's office. She has an 11 o'clock appointment.
5	**Grace**:	So what does that mean?
	Woman:	It's 10 till 11:00 right now.
	Grace:	So she wants to see me before?
	Woman:	Mm-hmm.
	Grace:	Uh … Virginia.
10	**Virginia**:	Yeah?
	Grace:	Anna wants to see us now … 'cause she has somewhere to be at 11:00.
	Virginia:	Okay. We're goin' in.

ANNA'S OFFICE 00:31:03-

15	**Grace**:	I have a ton of stuff here, and I don't know how many doubles, triples, singles I'm doing.	**a ton of stuff:** たくさんの
	Anna:	But maybe we can prioritize.	**prioritize:** 優先順位をつける
	Grace:	But, yeah. And you should, you know, if you hate something, just say "I never want to see that in the magazine."	
20			
	Anna:	Okay.	
	Grace:	Oh … there's two coats here. I'm … I'm sort of 5._____ about them. But I'm trying …	
	Anna:	It is 6._____ _____ the one we did in July.	
25	**Grace**:	It's not because you're thinking of the one we shot and 7._____ _____. I've shot them twice, but we have not had them in the magazine. The coat didn't run. Anyway, there's all these little dresses. And then there's a little coat. I love all these little evening things.	
30	**Anna**:	Let's remove the coat.	
	Grace:	I … I have to have a little freedom to 8._____ _____.	

	Anna:	Grace ... I mean, there's a lot of 9._____ things in this, and I want this to be more 9._____ than not.
	Grace:	I started working for American *Vogue* the same day as Anna did. I think we understand each other pretty much
5		... uh ... just through, you know, living together for twenty years. She knows I'm stubborn. I know she's stubborn, and I ... I know when to stop pushing her. Uh ... she doesn't know when to stop pushing me.
	Anna:	Is it odd just having one fur? I mean ... should we have
10		one other thing that has a fur? I mean ... I just think it's odd to have one. I mean, maybe you're going to do a fur hat or—
	Grace:	Okay.
	Anna:	I think it's sort of strange to have a whole shoot—
15	**Grace**:	I'm trying to make as many different looks as possible.
	Anna:	Yeah, but I think you need one more.
	Grace:	Otherwise, you're gonna get bored.
	Anna:	Well, I wouldn't ... I would take that out. And then these are all out, is that right?
20	**Grace**:	No. No. Absolutely not. These are beautiful. I mean ... Don't throw those out. They're beautiful.
	Anna:	And I don't think we should do this. It's the one from Resort, right?
	Grace:	Yeah, it's so perfect.
25	**Anna**:	I know, Grace. It's going in the stores in November. You can do it for the November issue.

VOGUE OFFICE 00:33:03–

	Grace:	How can she think of leaving these out?
	Virginia:	I know. I love those.
30	**Grace**:	That was unbelievable. But I'm not leaving them out.
	Virginia:	They're so cute.
	Grace:	Yeah, they are. And perfect. And what is this thing

Transcript

		about we need a fur coat to match that one?
	Virginia:	Or a fur hat.
	Grace:	Oh, please.
	Virginia:	[*laughs*]
5	**Grace**:	I mean, now, look. What's this? Or she's thrown it out. This is fur. This is fur. This is fur. That's the craziest thing I've heard.

LONG ISLAND, NEW YORK 00:33:39-

Interviewer: These are all the September issues …

10 **Bee**: Those are all the September issues …

Interviewer: that your mother …

	Bee:	… has done. Yeah. She had a lot of her old issues. And then one time, I came in here and looked and, like, saw that she didn't have everything that she'd ever done. And I just thought it would be nice for her. So now she's got everything.
15		
	Anna:	I remember that.
	Bee:	That was controversial.
	Anna:	That was controversial. Putting a black girl on the September cover was … for my first one, that was considered questionable. This got us a lot of attention, fur on the cover. This is the death-warmed-up cover.
20		
	Bee:	This one's really cute, there're puppies.
	Anna:	I know, but … They look … They look so pale. (*v/o*) I certainly read British *Vogue* when I was fourteen, fifteen. (*To Bee*) This is the one you hated.
25		
	Bee:	Yeah.
	Anna:	(*To the camera*) My American grandmother used to send me *Seventeen*. That was a very high point of my childhood every month. (*To Bee*) Oh, right, Gwyneth. This was when we moved into celebrities. So we've gotta decide between these two. Which one?
30		

warmed-up: 具合が悪い

Seventeen: 10代女性対象のアメリカのファッション雑誌

Bee: I like the color on that.

Anna: You do?

Bee: But I like the dress on the other one.

Anna: All right. And then the other thing I wanted to show you, darling, was—What do you think? That's got your look.

Bee: Her hair is in her face in that one.

Anna: You like that one?

Bee: One of these.

Anna: Okay, good.

Man: Do you think you'd ever work at the magazine with your mom?

Bee: No. I think I'm gonna go to law school. So probably not. [*chuckles*] But I don't know. I'm gonna get through college first. Sorry, Mommy.

Anna: Well, early days. We'll see.

(Speaking to camera – Bee) 00:35:41-

Bee: I really don't want to work in fashion. It's just not for me. I really respect her, obviously. Um … But it's a really weird industry to me, and it's just not for me. She wants me to be an editor. I don't wanna put it down, but it's … I would never wanna take it too seriously. Some of the people in there act like fashion is life. And it's just … It's really amusing, and you can make fun of them. But for that to be your career, it's just like … you know … There are other things out there, I think.

weird: 変な、奇妙な

Transcript

Unit 5
Six Weeks Until Closing

Ch. 5 00:36:16-00:46:14

André:	Isabel. Let's take a look at your Resort collection.	
Isabel:	They're very clean and crisp.	
André:	Almost—this is a compliment—institutional, clinical.	
Isabel:	You got it.	
5 **André**:	Clinical.	
Isabel:	You got it.	
Anna:	André …	
Woman:	André's having a great time with Isabel today. Fabulous time. Has all these ideas of still lives and things that we can do, so we're doing all that.	
10		
André:	You make sunglasses, too?	
Isabel:	Yeah.	
André:	Upside down.	
Isabel:	Look at my tape. Exactly.	
15 **André**:	Upside down. [*Chuckles*]	
Isabel:	You have such an eye.	

Woman:	Make sure you feature the bag.

Man:	It's very cinematic.
Anna:	I like that a lot.
20 **Man**:	Yeah, I really do.

Notes

crisp: こぎれいな、きちんとした

COLOR BLOCKING SHOOT 00:37:09-

Edward: Nice block. Beautiful.

Anna: This is it? I don't love the way these purple pants look, do you? They look … big. Are they sending more choices, or is this kind of it?

Man: The … These are all, you know … they gave me.

Grace: Somehow, you know, little dark wigs we've seen quite often, so you have to find another way to do a twenties. Do you like that?

Grace(*in a car*): The girls were 1._____, and … uh … they all seemed to work perfectly. I … I hope it looks as good as I think it does. We've done them in a very soft color. You know, it's almost like old film that's 2._____. I love when … when it goes soft and even sometimes if there's 3._____, there's a little blur and things, but … I don't know. Everybody seems to like things 4._____ these days. I think it's a 5._____.

blur: はっきりしないもの

GAP DESIGN EDITIONS THAKOON 00:38:33-

Thakoon: I hope it's okay.
Jane: I think this looks great.
Thakoon: Yeah.
Jane: Is that this week?
Thakoon: This was this morning.
Jane: This morning?
Thakoon: Yeah. I mean, I knew that they were doing ad, but I didn't know …
Jane: That that would be on the cover.
Thakoon: Right. It's kind of exciting.
Jane: I guess I would just … just start at the beginning with

Transcript

		the … when The Gap came to you.
	Thakoon:	It was *Vogue* that called and said that, you know, we are working with The Gap this coming-up year, and … you know … we want to launch the partnership with
5		this concept of reworking the white shirt idea.

	Woman:	Congrats.
	Thakoon:	Thank you.
	Woman:	Your face is everywhere. How are you?
	Woman:	It's good to see you.
10	**Thakoon**:	It's amazing. It's sick. It's sick.
	Woman:	Amazing. So proud of you. It's so great.
	Thakoon:	Hi, Anna, how are you?
	Anna:	Hi. So, I told you I'd get you The Gap.
	Thakoon:	I know, I know. You got me a huge thing, which is great.
15		Thank you so much.
	Anna:	It's so funny. I was thinking about our conversation all those months ago.
	Thakoon:	I know. I know. I keep thinking … I … I didn't realize it was gonna turn into such a big deal, but …
20	**Anna**:	Have you had a good response?
	Thakoon:	Yes. I think they were sold out online.
	Anna:	Really?
	Thakoon:	Yeah.
	Anna:	Great. Sorry.

25 **VOGUE OFFICE** `00:39:54-`

	Grace:	So this is what we shot the other day. It was really divine. This is all Galliano, who was the inspiration and the start of the whole story. But I completely fell in love with these. This is Coco. She was doing the Charleston
30		here on the bar, nearly fell off, but I think that's kinda great.

the Charleston:
1920年代にアメリカで流行したサウスカロライナ州のチャールストン市発祥のダンス
kinda=kind of

	Anna:	Excuse me.
	Woman:	Oh, sure.
	Charlie:	We're gonna try to print these out again brighter.
	Anna:	Okay. This one is a little unnecessary.
5	**Charlie**:	I know. It's another story.
	Anna:	Yeah. Don't you think?
	Charlie:	Yeah.
	Anna:	Too much.
	Charlie:	It is. It's all that posing, in different kind of a set almost.
10	**Anna**:	Yeah, but the others look fine. But do you agree?
	Charlie:	Yeah.
	Anna:	It looks fake.
	Charlie:	I think you have more personality out of these than you do on that, also.
15	**Anna**:	Mm … hmm. And there's plenty of Galliano, so …
	Charlie:	Yes. No, they're fun. Anna, this one's again, the group.
	Anna:	Yeah.
	Charlie:	But maybe if it's more in the middle, it might work.
	Anna:	We'll see.
20	**Charlie**:	All right.
	Anna:	How many are there?
	Charlie:	Twenty-two. Let me give you the right number.
	Anna:	They have a sort of haze over them, too.
	Charlie:	I … Okay. I have to find out how much—I'm gonna go
25		check and see how much of that is in the Xeroxing.
	Charlie:	I need to print out the beauty better for sure.
	Brian:	Yeah. Okay.
	Charlie:	And then try to print this out better too if you can.
	Brian:	Sure. Let's see if that helps it.
30	**Grace**:	Flat or soft?
	Charlie:	It's … it's … it's … the … Well, look.

haze: もや、かすみ

Xerox: ゼロックス（アメリカの印刷機器の製造販売会社）

flat: 単調な、深みがない

Transcript

	Grace:	Because they're meant to be …
	Charlie:	I think it's 'cause on the screen, there's a little bit more color. Now 'cause even in the beauty, that Meisel did, it's everything. I think it's just the printer right now. It's
5		the printer right now.
	Grace:	They're meant to be soft. They're meant to be.
	Charlie:	Okay.
	Grace:	That's the point.
	Charlie:	But the colors are not like this, though.
10	**Grace**:	Like this. No, they are.
	Charlie:	Right. I think that to be like that, no matter what.
	Grace:	I mean, they're meant to be. They're not supposed to be bright, you know, like this. They're not all like that.
	Charlie:	No. No. No, it's … I know that. No. No, I know.
15	**Grace**:	So don't try because you won't get anywhere.
	Charlie:	No. It's just seems …
	Grace:	I mean, you probably will, 'cause you can probably pump them up, but it's really a shame. This is out?
	Charlie:	Maybe.
20	**Grace**:	Are you kidding?
	Charlie:	No.
	Grace:	Why?
	Charlie:	Because she doesn't feel it goes with the rest of the story so much. Wait and see. This is early yet. We have
25		the whole issue to put together.
	Grace:	I … I don't get why it wouldn't go in. That … that's all Galliano, which is the point of the thing.
	Charlie:	You've got a few more.
	Grace:	Hum?
30	**Charlie**:	You've got a few more in there.
	Grace:	Yeah.
	Charlie:	I love these. It's wonderful, these.
	Grace:	It's astounding. No, they're supposed to be soft like

pump up: 自信・熱意などを注ぎ込む

Wait and see.: 成り行きを静観しましょう。

		that. They're supposed to be backlit. It's maybe all the things she doesn't like, but that's what they're supposed to be.
Charlie:		No, it's great. It's really nice. Thanks. I'll talk to her.

---

5 **Charlie**: Is this the run-through for Sienna?
Tonne: This is Sienna coming up.
Charlie: So I don't have to be there for that one.
Tonne: Well, it's a cover.
Charlie: I'll go … I'll go to it, sure. Just call me when.
10 **Tonne**: So …

SIENNA MILLER 00:43:28-

Sienna: Sorry about this. This is like a girly heaven.
Savannah: Holy crap.
Sienna: Oh, my God. Is that the Marchesa line?
15 **Savannah**: Oh, my God.
Sienna: It's amazing.
Savannah: That's amazing.
Sienna: Oh, my God.
Savannah: Is that wings? No.
20 **Woman**: It's Nina Ricci.
Sienna: Why … I don't understand how everyone sort of collectively does—Do they design them specially?
Woman: Yeah. I mean, it's the September issue of *Vogue*.

Anna: Hi, guys.
25 **Sienna**: Hi. Hello. How are you? I'm good.
Woman: Hello. Hi.
Sienna: This is Savannah, my sis.
Anna: Hi, I'm Anna. How are you? Thank you for coming.
Tonne: Do you wanna try that?
30 **Anna**: It looks cheap to me.

---

backlit: [backlightの過去分詞]…の背後から照明を当てる

Holy crap.:（驚きを表して）なんてことだ、ちょっと見て。
Marchesa: マルケッサ（NYのファッションブランド）

Nina Ricci: ニナ・リッチ（パリ創業のファッションブランド）

sis = sister

Transcript

Tonne: Okay, put it back.

Anna: That's quite ridiculous.

Tonne: The 6._____ for *Vogue* to putting celebrities on its covers has been because of Anna. She was 7._____ _____ _____ _____ to appreciate the fact that celebrity culture became overwhelming.

Sienna: 8._____ _____ _____ _____ pose in this bit?

Tonne: No, darling.

Sienna: I don't know ...

Sally: What *Vogue* did and what the supermodels did in the pages of *Vogue* is that they trained a generation of celebrities to want to be supermodels. Actresses 9._____ _____ that fashion was a seamless part of life and a seamless part of celebrity, and that was fine.

Anna: [*Gasps, Chuckles*]

Woman: Oh, my goodness.

Sienna: It's amazing. Really, no pasta. I can't bear going to Rome and not being able to have pasta. That's incredible.

Anna: It is. You 10._____ _____ in that.

Woman: Mmhmm.

Laurie: This is amazing. I thought it was in Paris. It's amazing.

Grace: [*Chuckles*]

Laurie: And the rest of the shoot is just brilliant, Grace.

Grace: Well. Do mention it to Anna because she's killed half of it.

Laurie: It's just beautiful. It is beautiful.

Phyllis: She took out the two best pictures.

Sienna: Tonne, do you wanna go talk to the hair stuff, or do you

seamless: 縫い目（継ぎ目）のない

		want to do that another time?
	Tonne:	You know what? I just wanted to show you this. This was what you … what we looked up, which I loved. It's divine, isn't it?
5	**Sienna**:	My hair's too thick to do it with.
	Tonne:	You're … You mean … You're great in short hair.
	Sienna:	Do you think better? Do you?
	Tonne:	I do. I mean … I have a survey of every hairstyle you've had for my board. I'm serious.
10	**Sienna**:	[*laughs*]
	Tonne:	The shoot is centered around a weekend in Rome. She's gonna go … um … around town and I have to storyboard that, literally. Because this is gonna be highly produced. Otherwise, it's gonna be chaos.
15		Feathers.
	Grace:	[*Coughing*]

Transcript

Unit 6
Day Before Paris

 Ch. 6 00:46:16-00:53:30

VOGUE OFFICE 00:46:16-

Anna:	I'm going to Europe today. Rome, Paris, and London.	
André:	What time are we leaving on Wednesday?	
Woman:	I'm emailing your itinerary, shortly.	
5 **André**:	Just tell me a time.	
Virginia:	Have we organized, like, where they would bring these dresses in Rome?	
Tonne:	No.	
Grace:	It's a problem when yours are the first pictures in.	
10	'Cause people get bored with them. So she's gonna love the Rome pictures, because they'll come straight in, and they'll go straight to press. So … If Sienna gets sick and doesn't turn up in Rome maybe, maybe all the pictures will come back [*Chuckles*]. They'll probably find	
15	another celebrity to take her place, I don't know.	
Anna:	So, shall we not talk about feathers anymore?	
Woman:	The feather discussion is over.	
Anna:	Okay. Is there anything we need to talk about for December, or is that just wait till we come back?	
20 **Virginia**:	I think we're done.	
Anna:	Grace, I'm leaving soon. Do you need me for anything?	
Grace:	Umm … Well, yeah, we have, uh … you know, like … Are there any restrictions on the Couture? The 1._____ is a problem, because, you know—	
25 **Anna**:	Christiane says the budget is fine.	

Notes

Grace: It's not fine. It's not fine. It's not that simple.

Anna: This is … Well, you need to talk with her because she has the 2._____.

Grace: I know, but it's a hell of a lot of work to put together, which I don't want to do if you have a 3._____ budget. So I can't really find out what the limit is … 'cause the limit keeps changing.

Now, I'm in a really 4._____ mood because they've killed a lot of the spread of my twenties story. And they're about to kill another one. And they're all lying to me about it, including Danko, who I thought was my friend. You just sit here and everything is killed. It's, like, incredibly 5._____. And I love to talk money in front of you guys with Anna … 'cause it drives her crazy. [*laughs*] It's a sure way to get the budget up.

Anna: I don't like this.

Charlie: No. Then I'll rid you of this, too. Good.

Anna: No. No, it's … it's … it's just that that's not a good place for that to go.

Charlie: Oh, okay.

Anna: This … this is too long, Charlie.

Charlie: Still.

Anna: I think it's a spread too long.

Charlie: All right, we'll take it down. It's easy to take down then, if that's the case.

Anna: Well I'm leaving, so …

Charlie: Yes, I'll have him do it right away.

Anna: Wait till I've gone.

Charlie: Okay.

a hell of: [形+名の前に置いて]とても、どえらい

drive someone crazy: …をいらいらさせる

take down: 取り下げる、除去する

Transcript

(On the phone) `00:49:08-`

Tonne: Didier? I'm fine. How are you? I think that it's actually going to be a wig, Didier, so you're gonna need time to, yeah. Mm … Hmm. Her hair is just completely lackluster, and … uh … she's growing it out. She won't cut it. You know, blah, blah, blah, blah, blah. It might be just easier to do a wig.

blah: [口語] ばかばかしい、くだらない

Anna: Do you need this?
Woman: And your tickets are in the July, your 'up' envelope.
Anna: Okay, and … um … what about money?
Woman: The money is in the bag.
Anna: Okay. Okay. See you guys in Europe. Bye.

Grace: And it will be more. Well, I think we have to discuss things.
Charlie: Anna's gonna be around until the next …
Grace: Until Tonne's pictures come in.
Charlie: She's come back.
Grace: And, you know …
Charlie: That's for next month.
Grace: No, Sienna is not next month.
Charlie: But we're not going to really do the issue until Anna gets back. We're just putting all these things up.
Grace: Well, no, you're taking them all down. You're taking everything down. They took two more out, and there's 6._____ marks on two more. So it's been 7._____ _____ and I'm furious. They've probably thrown out $50,000 8._____ of work. I care very much about what I do. I do, or I 9._____ be still doing it, you know. Um … But it gets harder and harder to see it just 10._____ out. [*pause*] And it's very hard to go onto the next thing.

Paris - Gaultier 00:51:50-

Anna: How are you, Grace? Hi, how are you? Did they give you the message about Chanel?

Grace: That you're going this afternoon?

5 **Anna**: Yeah.

Grace: Yeah. Yeah.

Anna: Jean Paul.

Jean: How are you, Anna? Nice to see you.

Anna: Nice to see you, too.

10 **Jean**: Pleasure to see you. Welcome … welcome to Paris. All right. Uh … Maybe I want, the thing is that my clothes—

Anna: Nothing's ready. You're gonna say the usual story.

Jean: Bon. But, but, but, but, but, but, but we are still going to show you.

15 **Woman**: Is she there?

Jean: I show you the only one you can see. Coco? Voilà.

Anna: Coco, how was you?

Jean: The dress is not done. The dress is not done, but it will be like "the dress" like "fer forgé", you know. The

20 collection is different prince of different countries.

Woman: Wow.

Bon: [仏]=Good

fer forgé: [仏]錬鉄（炭素含有量を少なくした鉄）

Transcript

Unit 7
Paris Couture

Ch. 7   00:53:31-01:02:22

Grace: Well, you know, I'm doing a shoot here in Paris. I mean, I'm looking, 'cause I always come to the Couture, almost always. I've been actually for twenty years at American *Vogue* and twenty years before that on British
5   *Vogue* and a few years before that when I was modeling. So I've been coming for a long time. Obviously, ostensibly, I'm there to find something to shoot. But I always mark too many things. [*laughs*] Anna says, 'Don't be silly. We can't do that one.' But,
10   uh …

LONDON 00:54:56-

Anna: Hi, darling. How are you?
Mario: I'm good, and you?
Anna: Did you see the match last—
15   **Mario:** My God, you look amazing for this room.
Anna: [*laughs*] Right. I didn't think. Did you see Roger's match yesterday?
Mario: He won. No, I didn't see it, but I heard he won. So, we go to Sienna. So a schedule, a rough schedule I've
20   done with Tonne. Basically, I wanna create a film, you know. A mixture of Fellini meets Visconti meets …
Anna: Oh, right.
Mario: Almost like cinema—
Anna: *Roman Holiday.*
25   **Mario:** Yeah. Very … very cinematic. I think that I would like to

Notes

Fellini: フェリーニ（1920-93、イタリアの映画監督）
Visconti: ヴィスコンティ(1906-76、イタリアの映画監督）

		try and do a—
	Anna:	But the charming side of Italian film, rather than the broody, moody side.
	Mario:	Of course …
5	**Anna**:	Okay.
	Mario:	… but look how beautiful, her with the people in the background.
	Anna:	Yeah. Yeah.
	Mario:	I mean, I want things that are quite spectacular. And I want to do something to do with the Vespas in St. Peter's Square. And then I wanted something with horses and soldiers. I mean, there is a lot of white. Like, I love that.
	Anna:	Mm … hmm …
15	**Mario**:	The feeling of white. There's the pastry shop, which is all white. I mean, there's a lot of white. I don't know why I keep on looking at things that are white. You know, the white horses. Because I think that that would be good use for this too. And then I love this idea of putting the horse in odd places as well.
	Anna:	But I just don't want that to be the whole thrust of the story.
	Mario:	Yeah. Okay.
	Anna:	Now, let's, look, and talk about her, because her hair is not looking its best. And, I got to … she's …
	Mario:	We had thought of putting her … putting a wig on her. Like a little blond wig.
	Anna:	Well, I think that's a great idea.
	Mario:	A really graphic one.
30	**Anna**:	Yeah, blond. I mean … my advice, since we're going to be short on time, is if we decide on a look and just stay with it because …
	Mario:	Of course.

broody: 陰気な

Vespa: ヴェスパ（イタリアのピアッジオ製スクーター）
St. Peter's Square: ローマのサン・ピエトロ広場

pastry shop: 洋菓子屋

graphic: 目立つ

be short on time: 時間が足りない

Transcript

Anna:	… you don't wanna waste hours.	
Mario:	Oh, no. I would do a look, and that's her look.	
Anna:	Yeah.	
Mario:	Oh. Great. I'm really excited about this.	
5 **Anna**:	This is gonna be the biggest one in our history.	
Mario:	It is an amazing room, no?	
Anna:	Incredible. You should have a party here.	
Mario:	What, the September one is gonna be the—What, how many pages, like 10,000?	
10 **Anna**:	I don't know yet but it's the biggest in our history, so.	
Mario:	Really?	
Anna:	Yep. So we're excited.	
Mario:	I should have a party here, no?	

(Speaking to camera- Grace) `00:57:31-`

15 **Grace**: Paris is so beautiful. It really is. I never 1._____ to be a model or never, never dreamt to be a fashion editor. But I just loved the pages and the pictures. In my early years as a fashion editor, uh … I worked with Norman Parkinson, who was a really big 2._____. And he
20 taught me to always keep your eyes open, you know, never go to sleep in the car or anything like that. Keep watching, because whatever you see out the window or wherever, it can 3._____ you.

It is amazing. It's … it's sort of strange to think how old
25 it is. It's beautiful. I think I got 4._____ _____ somewhere, 'cause I'm, you know, still 5._____ _____. You have to go charging ahead. You can't stay behind.

Norman Parkinson:
ノーマン・パーキンソン
（ファッションや人物写真の分野を代表するイギリスの写真家）

COUTURE SHOOT `00:59:30-`

30 **David**: Okay. She looks good.

Grace: Good. Move her head just a tiny bit forward so you get like an 's.'

David: That ... Good. That's the one. Good. Good.

Grace: Oh, wow.

5 **ROME – SIENNA MILLER COVER SHOOT** 00:59:46-

Tonne: Anna? How are you? We're doing very well. I'm sitting here with Mario and everybody. Sienna's here. We're doing a wig. Everything's great.

Mario: Let's 6._____ our story like this. Let's do four visual
10 locations. Let's say …

Tonne: That's pretty 7._____, don't you think?

Mario: Yeah.

Tonne: I mean, look. You've got the Colosseum.

Mario: It is beautiful.

15 **Tonne**: It's beautiful.

Mario: I think we don't need it.

Tonne: It's got beautiful open-8._____ light. I mean, it's so pretty.

Mario: That is what I'm wondering: whether we want pretty. I
20 find I've done this hair, like, really — I would love something new. A new proposition.

Woman: Yeah.

Tonne: We tried the wig, and it did not work. And we 9._____. And we moved on in the right 10._____, I
25 think.

Mario: There, wow. Stay there. Don't move. Don't move. This is your face. Don't move. This is really beautiful, no? I like that freshness. It says September cover.
Go, Sienna. Come. Come. Come. Come. Come. Come.
30 Come. Come. Come. Come.
Okay, again. Go, go, go, go, go. And again. Come forward. Come forward. Go there.

Colosseum: コロセウム（ローマの円形闘技場）

proposition: 提案

Transcript

	Tonne:	That's quite beautiful. Isn't it, Mario?
	Mario:	No. I'm not convinced of this. Do we want her like this, is this good? Huh?
5	**Tonne**:	I can certainly get rid of the head thing. Do you wanna get rid of the head thing?
	Mario:	Maybe. Maybe it's not good.

COUTURE SHOOT 01:01:25-

	Raquel:	Grace, thanks for the pie. I just don't know if I should eat that … 'cause the corsets are so tight.
10	**Grace**:	It's … um … That's not going to make a difference, Raquel.
	Woman:	Hello.
	Grace:	There. Fantastico. Can you breathe? Are you all right?
	Raquel:	Yeah. Yeah.
15	**Grace**:	That's incredible. That's beautiful. And the expression here is very lovely.
	David:	Just play with your hands a little, Raquel, for me. There. Oh, wow.
	Grace:	Oh, wow. That's beautiful.
20	**David**:	It ain't bad.
	Grace:	I think you got it.
	David:	Okay. Come on.
	Grace:	Let's go. Thanks.
	David:	Well done, Raquel.
25	**Grace**:	[*make high pitch sound*]
	Raquel:	Mmm. [*chuckles*]

Fantastico. [伊] : = Fantastic.

ain't: [口語] is notの短縮形

Transcript

Unit 8
André Plays Tennis

Ch. 8 01:02:23-01:11:40

TENNIS COURT 01:02:23-

Man: Let's go, André, left, left.

André: Aw. Ms. Wintour inaugurated me into health by intervention. She saved my life, I guess, in the long-term because she intervened about three years ago that I got to lose the weight. So, naturally, what Ms. Wintour says goes. So I took up tennis.

Man: Over your shoulder. Come on. Come on. Come on. Good.

André: I wouldn't come to the tennis court in just a pair of shorts and a tennis shirt. I go to Damon Dash for my trousers. I go to Ralph Lauren for the shirts. This is my version of a tennis watch. It's a Piaget from the sixties. But I would wear this to the tennis court. I would wear it all day long. It's all a part of the whole life of being who I am. I have to get up and approach life with my own aesthetics about … style.

ONE WEEK UNTIL ISSUE CLOSES 01:03:29-

Woman: Anna Wintour's office.

Tom: The magazine will be actually almost nine million up when we come out of September.

Anna: Wonderful.

Sally: This is not a great-looking opener. I mean, this is a cleaner opener. You know, the girl looking at you. You wanna open with something people wanna read, I think.

Notes

man=tennis coach

intervention：介入、干渉

Damon Dash：デイモン・ダッシュ率いるNYの大人気ブランド
Ralph Lauren：ラルフ・ローレン(アメリカン・トラディショナル[アメトラ]の代表的存在であるファッションブランド)
Piaget：ピアジェ(スイスの時計とジュエリーの高級ブランド)

Transcript

	Anna:	Do you need me, Charlie?
	Charlie:	Yes, uh … the Couture's here.
	Anna:	Oh, great. What about Mario? [*chuckles*]
	Charlie:	Mario? He is … The film is on a plane and they don't
5		land until two.
	Grace:	Hello? I love them. They look gorgeous. I've stolen
		them. I snatched them out of Charlie's hands. [*laughs*]
		He went bu-bu-bu-bu-bu-bu-bu-bu-bu. [*laughs*]
		Kind of, but, you know, he … he hates to say until
10		Anna's seen them in case he makes a mistake.
	Anna:	A lot of wigs.
	Charlie:	All through it. It's fourteen pages.
	Anna:	This is pretty.
	Man:	Okay. That is fine. Thank you.
15	**Anna**:	Beautiful. Well, we can wait, right?
	Charlie:	Oh, yes, sure.
	Anna:	This slightly hinges on what happened with Sienna, I
		think.
	Charlie:	Okay.
20	**Anna**:	And … and Grace wasn't crazy about that one anyway.
	Charlie:	Hi. I know it, just … Brian just told me. It's … it's coming
		out now. So as soon as I look at it— Maybe I'll call you
		right back. Okay, thanks a lot, Mario. Okay. I need these
		printed out right away.
25	**Brian**:	Sure. Yeah, it's printing now, but—uh …
	Anna:	So this is what Mario sent?
	Charlie:	This is what he just sent, yes.
	Anna:	But did he … did he send the cover?
	Charlie:	No.
30	**Anna**:	Okay.

Charlie: Uh ... It's taking him a while to do that.

Anna: That's it?

Charlie: Yes.

Anna: That's it for the clothes?

5 **Charlie**: That's all I've gotten. That's all he said ... for now.

Anna: Can you get Tonne in here? I just ... it seems like ...

Charlie: I don't know if she's in yet. She wasn't in before. Let me see if she's back. Not yet. Her assistant's calling her to find out.

10 **Anna**: Okay. Could ... could we ask her assistant to see how many pictures here we're ... we're missing?

Man: Yes.

Charlie: This is all he sent.

Anna: Can I see Ivan, please?

15 **Man**: Ivan?

Anna: And I need Tonne's assistant or ... uh ... Hi. Did he say this was, there's more coming or there's nothing else?

Ivan: No, this, I think, is the story. But I'll go back to them and just double-check.

20 **Anna**: All right.

Ivan: As I understand it, this is everything.

Anna: Okay. Can we get Tonne's assistant or Virginia in here, please?

Anna: Tonne, I'm sorry, I'm losing you. I thought we were
25 gonna have more clothes.

Charlie: Okay, Mario. I'd like to see the rest of the film as soon as possible. You understand?

Anna: But I didn't get the Colosseum.

Charlie: Right. I don't think that's it. I think ... I think the thing is
30 ... is the whole look is everything. Truthfully.

Anna: It's a bit short on clothes.

Charlie: But I don't know if we even need to reshoot. But ... um

Truthfully.: 正直に言えば。

Transcript

	… it's something that's being talked about. So I just wanna put it in your ear. I just finished talking to Mario. No other Nina Ricci.
Anna:	That was it.
5 **Charlie**:	That was it.
Anna:	They didn't do it for me?
Charlie:	No. And they didn't—He says he didn't do the Colosseum dress. He says he didn't like it, so they didn't do it.
10 **Anna**:	Okay.

TONNE'S OFFICE 01:07:17-

Charlie:	I just finished 1._____ to Mario.
Tonne:	Yeah.
Charlie:	He says there is nothing on the dress at the Colosseum.
15 **Tonne**:	Well, he didn't like it. He really couldn't.
Charlie:	He says he didn't like it, so he never really did it, he said …
Tonne:	But, he …
Charlie:	… which I had to tell her.
20 **Tonne**:	He … You know, it's digital.
Charlie:	I know.
Tonne:	He did something, but he never got an image that he wanted 2._____ _____ _____.
Charlie:	Right.
25 **Tonne**:	You know, I understand that, you know, she needs a few more dresses but, you know, you get what you get.
Charlie:	I'm concerned a little 'cause I'm not 3._____ _____ _____ the cover at the moment. The one he's chosen, she's kind of tough-looking in the face.
30 **Tonne**:	Right.
Charlie:	That's not a face for a cover.
Tonne:	Right.

tough-looking: こわもてな、厳しそうな

	Charlie:	See this.
	Tonne:	Yeah. I mean …
	Charlie:	This … It can't be that.
5	**Tonne**:	I mean, I think there could be 4._____ be something there.
	Charlie:	That's what I think.
	Tonne:	So I … I think that's pretty 5._____.
	Charlie:	Well. Look at it now. I've cropped in on it and turned it.
	Tonne:	What does it say? Something.
10	**Charlie**:	[*sighs*] And …
	Tonne:	'Like this best, but teeth.'
	Charlie:	'But teeth.'

Anna: Mario. Hi. I just meant to ask if there was something there that you thought that we could at least look at.
15 Not one?

BEE'S HOUSE 01:08:24-

Anna: Florence, could you make me some coffee, please?

Florence: Okay.

Anna: Thank you. She … she has to look so conservative
20 because she's working at a lawyer's office.

Florence: No, a judge.

Anna: Judge. Sorry. My older brother is in charge of finding lower income housing in London for people that need it, and my sister's very involved in, uh … uh …
25 supporting farmers' rights in Latin America. My younger brother is … uh … political editor of *The Guardian*, and very successful, very brilliant. And, um … uh … My … my two brothers and my sister, um … I think they're very amused by what I do. Um … they're … They're
30 amused. So. All right. Well, have a good day.

Bee: See you.

judge: 裁判官、判事

Transcript

Anna: You, too.

Bee: Love you.

VOGUE OFFICE 01:10:15-

Sarah: Amanda Lacey is a London facialist who is a great friend of Plum's, and she's got a beautiful line of products, and she's opening a new store in London. And if it's ready, I'd love to do a little item on that. And then this is a piece … um … about all the advancements in eyes. And I think that eyes are something that women of all ages think about because their eyes start aging. They're the first thing that starts to age, and I think even women in their 20s are concerned about it, so …

Man: This is the look that André would prefer to have.

Anna: There's no alternative?

Man: There's um …

Anna: I said I didn't want any more …

Man: Environment?

Anna: Black and white.

Man: Black and white, okay. Is it this one, Anna, do you think?

Anna: Yeah, but I still like this one. Okay, but stronger. I remember when my dad 6._____, and I asked him why he was leaving because he was obviously so 7._____ _____ what he was doing still. And he said, 'Well, I get too angry. I get too angry and I 8._____ _____ _____ too angry.' So I do remember that, because I know there are times I get quite angry. So I try and 9._____ that. So I think when I 8._____ _____ _____ really, really angry, that might be 10._____ _____ _____.

Amanda Lacey: アマンダ・レイシー（ロンドンのスキンケア・セラピスト）
facialist: フェイシャリスト

Transcript

Unit 9
Grace Reflects

 Ch. 9 01:11:41-01:15:59

Grace:	It's very long Sienna. Twenty-two pages. Wow. Anna saw the celebrity thing coming way before everybody else ₁._____ on that bandwagon. And, you know, whilst I hated it, I … I … I'm afraid I have to ₂._____ she was right. You know, you can't … you can't stay behind. You have to go charging ahead. And … and … and she did, and the magazine is very ₃._____ because of it. I mean, whilst I'd be … I wouldn't really care if I never saw another celebrity. ₄._____ if the magazine doesn't sell, I don't have a job, so [*laughs*]. It would be silly. [*pause*] You know, you gotta have something to put your work in, otherwise it's not ₅._____.	**whilst:**[米方言] =while

FIVE DAYS UNTIL ISSUE CLOSES 01:13:17-

Woman: *Vogue*. Good morning.
Woman: Has Prada gotten this request yet or no?
Woman: I haven't heard back from them.

Grace: It's all change. [*chuckles*]
Woman: What?
Grace: It's all change.
Woman: What's all change?
Grace: The ₆._____ we're doing this weekend is going to be a reshoot of the color block shoot that Edward did.
Woman: What?

Transcript

Grace: Anna killed color blocking. And they, they wanna 7._____ it and then, but, of course, it's very 8._____, so …

Charlie: I got your message. We're already working on it.
Anna: Okay.
Charlie: A little while.
Anna: Okay.

Grace: I've gotta get all new clothes in five minutes.
Woman: Okay.
Grace: It's getting a little busy up here.
Woman: There's just a bunch on the 9._____ rack. I don't know where it came from.
Man: Sarah has Marc Jacobs on her 10._____. I'll grab that for you as well.

Grace: What about stuff like this?
Virginia: That particular one was shot, but, yes, in theory, it could be color blocked.
Grace: But I shot one of these in that same issue, so that's no good. And this one?
Virginia: That's good. That hasn't been shot.
Grace: Have I shot that skirt?
Virginia: You shot the skirt. Yes.

Laurie: This has to close on Thursday.
Charlie: I know.
Laurie: And it's not gonna come in until Wednesday?
Charlie: Now, Laurie, I … I can't do anything about it. Just … a change was made, and I didn't even know.

Grace: Did I shoot this? I shot this.

up here: ここまで

bunch: 束

Marc Jacobs: マーク・ジェイコブス（アメリカのファッションブランド）

Virginia: You did.

Grace: There's a red coat.

Virginia: Yes. Shot. Was your twenties Prada dress shot? The red one?

5 **Grace**: Yeah.

Virginia: You shot it, and … and it … it was—

Grace: And it was killed.

Charlie: We just redid the layout.

Mario: I feel very excited to see that there was a photo of mine
10 in the hallway. Twenty years later. [*laughs*] Are we opening the issue?

Charlie: Yes, as of now.

Mario: What do you mean 'as of now'? Doesn't it have to ship? [*laughs*] Is that all I did?

15 **Charlie**: That's all.

Mario: I seemed to, like, sweat, like, mad to get these.

Charlie: Whatever happened to the Colosseum, I don't know. That was the only one. But …

Mario: That didn't work, unfortunately. You know we had little
20 time, and I wanted to do another cover, and I said, you know, I'm not gonna spend three hours here.

Charlie: Right.

Mario: I would rather do a cover. Do you have the covers?

Charlie: Right here. It's between these two. We're testing both
25 for now.

Mario: Do you think I should use this body and that head?

Charlie: Let's look, let's do this.

Mario: Would this be more—

Charlie: It's a better neck.

30 **Mario**: No?

Charlie: We have to retouch a lot of this because it's a lot of teeth. It's very teethy.

redid: [redoの過去形]やり直す

hallway: (ビルの)玄関、入口

as of now: 今のところ、今現在

sweat: いらだつ、苦しむ
like mad: [口語]激しく

	Mario:	Mm … hmm.
	Charlie:	And also there's a filling, there's a couple of fillings there.
	Mario:	Mm … hmm.
5	Charlie:	But we can fix that.
	Mario:	Of course. Yeah. Yeah. Absolutely. I think that that is very inviting.
	Charlie:	You know, when we put cover lines on there, it's gonna be at you.
10	Mario:	Yeah.
	Charlie:	So that's the one. But I … you're right. I think that neck—
	Mario:	That shoulder is boring. Might be more beautiful, no?
	Charlie:	And I'm gonna dummy it up that way, so.
15	Mario:	Okay, great.
	Charlie:	All right.

dummy up:(印刷物の)束[割付]見本を作る

Transcript

Unit 10
Color Block, Take Two ~ End Credits

Ch. 10-12　01:16:00-01:29:48

Woman:	Okay …	
Grace:	There's no color stuff left that hasn't already been shot that is any good, so …	
Laurie:	So, what … What is it called that you're shooting?	
5　**Grace**:	I don't know. [*laughs*] I'm making it up as I go along. Whoops. And I've got two days to …	
Laurie:	Is this the last shoot that … that we expect?	
Grace:	You'd better pray it is, because otherwise I don't know who's gonna shoot it.	
10　**Laurie**:	Uh … the biggest issue of the year, and we have to close, and they're still shooting.	
Grace:	No, I had an idea, but I don't know if I want to do it or not, and it involves you. That's why I'm asking. Not you, Tonne. My friend here. [*laughs*]	

15　**COLOR BLOCKING RESHOOT**　01:16:40-

Patrick:	How do you feel today? Good? You feel young today? Feel good?
Bob:	I feel great.
Patrick:	Yeah. We have a little plan for you. [*chuckles*]
20　**Grace**:	Can you jump?
Patrick:	Yeah, that's great, very fun. This was great. Uh … one more … one more, okay? Okay.
Grace:	Oh. That's great.
Patrick:	So we want her on the same page, very close to him,

whoops: おっと、しまった　※間違いなどをした時の驚きや軽い詫びの気持ちを表す

		like that?	
	Grace:	Right.	
	Patrick:	Jumping, too.	
	Grace:	That's good, I think. She's looking right in the lens.	
5	**Patrick**:	Yeah. Yeah. Good.	
	Brian:	Here we go. Awesome.	**Awesome**: [口語] すごい、すげえ
	Charles:	How many times did they make you jump?	
	Bob:	Not too many.	
	Anna:	I like them. They're fun. I mean, we just needed a breath	
10		of fresh air in the issue. Everything was quite dense. So	
		… They look great. Wearable, accessible, great props.	
		We're working on this one.	
	Bob:	Yeah.	
	Anna:	A little bit of … a little bit of retouching. Need to go to	**retouch**: 画像を修正する
15		the gym.	
	Virginia:	[*laughs*] Anna.	
	Anna:	But they look great. I'm glad we redid it.	
	Sally:	It's Patrick?	
	Anna:	Patrick, yes.	
20	**Sally**:	Great.	
	Anna:	Patrick and Grace.	

	Grace:	Did she like them?	
	Bob:	"A bit of retouching," she said.	
	Grace:	Oh, I bet. [*laughs*] Of course.	**I bet**=I'm sure
25	**Bob**:	She told me I needed to go to the gym.	
	Grace:	Uh … 1._____ _____ which picture? The jumping one?	
	Bob:	Yeah. She's right.	
	Grace:	No, but, it … I … you know, 2._____, I think it's	
30		better that you're not, like, skinny, skinny. I really … To	**skinny**: やせこけた

me, it's much more, makes ₃_____ _____ than
… that you're real people and not … models.
Everybody isn't ₄_____ in this world. I mean, it's
enough that the models are ₄_____. You don't
need to go to the gym. [*laughs*]

Bob: Thank you, Grace.

Grace: Charlie? When you are looking at Patrick's pictures, please do not retouch Bob's stomach. No, please don't, because I don't want him to look like, you know, a skinny male model. Okay. But … no … I just wanted to catch his stomach before you gave him a—He's pulling it in now as I speak. [*laughs*] Uh … Okay. All right. Thanks, bye. Phew.

Phew.: ふーっ。
※苛立ち・不快・驚きなどを表す

MEETING ROOM AND SEVERAL LOCATIONS AT OFFICE

01:20:38-

(*Everyone cheers and claps hands*)

Tom: We are one-hundred pages up over last year. In one issue.
Anna: I'd better go and finish it.
Tom: Me, too.
Man: Enjoy, guys.
Man: So make it good now.

Virginia: Twenties, and color block, polished.
Anna: And then what about her teeth?
Charlie: Oh, I've been working on this a lot. I'm gonna fix her neck. So that's the new neck.
Brian: Yeah. It's the better covers.
Charlie: Okay.
Man: This is the new neck on this.
Man: Okay, great.

Transcript

	Sally:	So, we have to write "Sienna Miller" large, or people won't know. If this is right, you can't write 'Singular Sienna' or 'Sensational Sienna.'
	Anna:	This all seems so large and pretentious, this type.
5	**Man**:	Um … hmm. Okay.
	Anna:	Looks like it's for blind people.
	André:	It's going to come out like that, right?
	Laurie:	Is she wearing feathers? Are those feathers? What are we supposed to do with feathers this fall?
10	**Sally**:	You are supposed to wear them. [*laughs*]
	Woman:	And then there's a ring.
	Anna:	These aren't very good.
	Charlie:	No.
	Man:	This is not in the correct order.
15	**Charlie**:	Yes, it is.
	Anna:	More like this.
	Man:	Okay. Yeah. Exactly.

blind: 目の不自由な

SEPTEMBER ISSUE CLOSING 01:21:53-

	Charlie:	Do we have the book and the cover there?
20	**Anna**:	Is everything updated?
	Brian:	Yes, Anna.
	Anna:	Hum?
	Brian:	Okay.

MEETING ROOM 01:22:07-

25	**Anna**:	Then this is our cover girl whom we took to Rome with Mario Testino. She … uh … was interviewed here by

	Sally Singer. We … uh … had the idea to do a sort of Jazz Age shoot. That's … uh … Thakoon, and … uh … on the right is Chanel. And that is the issue.
Man:	Very nice, Anna.
Anna:	Thank you.

Grace:	Oh, my God. Wasn't Sienna originally the lead? Yes, it was. [*sighs*] Okay. Just one more spread here.
Man:	The … the …
Grace:	Then it will be my whole issue just about, except for Sienna.

Tom:	It looks great.

Anna:	Fashion's not about looking back. It's always about looking forward. Okay, next.
Brian:	Sorry.
Anna:	Move the board. [*chuckles*]
Brian:	Yes, we will.

| **Anna**: | [*To the interviewer*] I don't believe for one minute that I have ₅._____ _____ _____ what's gonna happen or ₅._____ _____ _____ real change the way Grace does. I mean, Grace's a ₆._____, and there is no one that can visualize a picture or understand the … the ₇._____ of fashion or … produce a great shoot. I mean, she's just ₈._____. [*To her assistant*] Okay. [*To the interviewer*] She and I don't always agree, but I think that over the years we've learned how to ₉._____ _____ each other's different ₁₀._____ _____ _____. |

Woman: Anna Wintour's office.

Jazz Age: ジャズ・エイジ⇒p. 68参照

Anna: Is anyone coming to this run-through except for me? So what else?

END CREDIT 01:24:35-

Man: You know you're featured in the September issue?
Thakoon: [*chuckles*] No way.
Woman: He was gonna walk to the newsstand and get the surprise. [*laughs*]
Thakoon: When is it coming out?

André: Is this better? This is authority. This is it or nothing.
Man: [*laughs*] Let me see.
André: This is it or nothing, okay? When I got the pose, strike it.

Grace: That was a stroke of genius on my side, I think. I turned the cameras on you. And it just came to me, like, I … I was walking along the corridor, and I was like, 'Oh, my God, they're looking at my rack again.' And, I can't … 'Hang on a minute.' I'll teach them. [*laughs*]

Man: What's your strength?
Anna: Decisiveness.
Man: Your weakness?
Anna: My children.
Man: What gift would you like?
Anna: A better backhand.

(END)

---

strike it: ポーズをとる Cf. strike a pose「ポーズをとる」

stroke: 一撃 Cf. stroke of genius「天才的発想」

corridor: 廊下

JPCA 本書は日本出版著作権協会（JPCA）が委託管理する著作物です。
複写（コピー）・複製、その他著作物の利用については、事前に JPCA（電話 03-3812-9424, e-mail:info@e-jpca.com）の許諾を得て下さい。なお、無断でコピー・スキャン・デジタル化等の複製をすることは著作権法上
日本出版著作権協会 の例外を除き、著作権法違反となります。
http://www.e-jpca.com/

The September Issue
映画総合教材『ファッションが教えてくれること』

2017 年 4 月 10 日　初版第 1 刷発行
2024 年 4 月 2 日　初版第 3 刷発行

編著者　　板倉厳一郎／野村昌司／Suzanne Bonn／志賀奈月美

発行者　森　信久
発行所　株式会社　松　柏　社
〒 102-0072　東京都千代田区飯田橋 1-6-1
TEL 03 (3230) 4813（代表）
FAX 03 (3230) 4857
http://www.shohakusha.com
e-mail: info@shohakusha.com

装　　幀　小島トシノブ（NONdesign）
本文レイアウト　株式会社クリエーターズ・ユニオン（一柳 茂）
印刷・製本　中央精版印刷株式会社
ISBN978-4-88198-722-3
略号＝ 722

Copyright © 2017 by Gen'ichiro Itakura, Masashi Nomura, Suzanne Bonn, Natsumi Shiga
本書を無断で複写・複製することを禁じます。
落丁・乱丁は送料小社負担にてお取り替え致します。